Why pink elephants? Well it's a psychological thing. If I say 'Don't think about pink elephants' what do you think about? What are you thinking about now? Pink elephants right? It's about the way the mind works. You have to think about it in order to not think about it. Also, it is thought that the unconscious mind (where your behaviour patterns are created) does not compute certain negative words such as don't. Therefore, the phrase becomes a command to 'Think about pink elephants.' This may be why if you tell kids or teenagers or other annoying people not to do things it becomes the thing they most want to do. Don't make noise. Don't drink a lot. Don't speak to me like that. Don't touch me. Don't behave like an idiot etc.

Don't Think About Pink Elephants

Peter Gilmour

Simple, Rapid, Effective Techniques for
Confidence, Energy, Success and Happiness

'The only self-help book you will ever need'

Published in Great Britain by Placebo Publishing
3, St Gabriel's Manor, 25 Cormont Road, London SE5 9RH

A catalogue record of this title is available from The British Library

ISBN: 978-1-9160448-0-7

Design by Viktor David

Illustrations by Peggy Prendeville

Printed by CLOC printers, Tottenham Hale, London

For Peggy, Shelley and Josh

The author would like to thank Viktor David for the cover design and also his expert, invaluable computer and graphic work. Charles Harris and Michael Foster for reading the book and offering very welcome advice and encouragement. Georgina, Joel and Josh for being models for the various sketches. Peggy for drawing the sketches. Special thanks must also go to Simon and Andrew (the boys), Mick, Dolf, Bernie, Mo, Maz, Carlos, Ray, Bernadette, Bob and Paul for their help and continuing belief in my work. And Peggy again for simply being Peggy and the inspiration behind everything I do.

Table of Contents

Preface

Magical Mystery Methods

There is no real mystery. It just seems like it because of the way we are. The way we're disconnected from the natural flow of energy. The way we exist somewhere deep in the sub-strata of existence on a parallel stream to that of the essential life forces that would undoubtedly allow us to be happy and fulfilled in the warm sunshine of love if we only knew how to connect with them. Occasionally there's a flash. An epiphany that allows us a brief glimpse of something lurking somewhere in the shadows that would allow us to understand the nature of being if we could just lift our consciousness long enough to focus on it properly. It holds out a promise of peace and serenity and love and fulfilment and much as we yearn for this beautiful dream it always seems to remain just beyond us. A tantalising vision just ever so slightly out of reach.

Some are quite certain that the time will come when we'll be able to immerse ourselves in the positive energy of this vision albeit probably only in the life hereafter which is fine for them. They talk about life after death but I prefer to focus on life before death. To create Shangri-La right here and now. To live now and to love now and to be joyful now and to understand everything now and of course, to live forever. Now.

Having delved into these metaphysical concepts for many years I have discovered beyond doubt that that whoever you are, wherever you are, whatever you do, there are quite a number of simple, rapid, potent techniques you can utilise to feel great, be happy, achieve your ambitions, raise your consciousness and improve your life in every way right now. Yes, right now. Guaranteed. Yes, Guaranteed.

Over the years I have scoured the world to find methods of many different kinds from many different cultures to help many different people in many different ways. As someone who is known for highly specialised work at the top level of sport I have principally sought techniques to prepare the athlete's mind for competition but what emerges beyond doubt is that all the amazing methods I have discovered and developed for use with athletes and which I describe in the pages of this book can be utilised by anyone at all in order to enhance their lives in any way they need or desire. It's all about energy and when you master the technique of stimulating your energy to flow easily and effortlessly then anything and everything becomes possible. And of course everything is connected to everything else. Naive as it may sound, my mission is to take these methods, techniques and modalities out into the world and pass them on to as many folk as possible in order to create a happier, healthier and more loving world with the fervent hope that it will bring us closer to the vision we chase.

My strong recommendation to the authorities everywhere is that the methods here should be used every day for about five to ten minutes in various places such as: Schools and universities to promote a healthier and more vibrant learning environment. In the corporate sector to create more happiness in the workplace, team-bonding and better productivity. In hospitals for patients to enjoy a faster recovery and for the staff to have better energy to help them. In any branches of sport, the arts and entertainment to boost mental focus, confidence, belief and enhance performance levels. For the millions suffering from stress, anxiety, fear, doubt, worry etc. to feel better and happier as they overcome the vagaries of our difficult and dysfunctional, modern society.

If you can take a little leap of faith with me into the magic world of energy psychology, I promise you'll find it very rewarding not to say totally inspirational.

Peter's Panacea

'The greatest danger for most of us is not that our aim is too high and we miss it, but that it is too low and we reach it.' - Michaelangelo

Imagine you had an instant switch for happiness. A switch that eliminated stress, anxiety, fear, doubt and worry and allowed you to enjoy a life full of happiness and fulfilment. Wouldn't that be amazing? Well that's what you get with this book. A range of simple, rapid, potent techniques that instantly switch on your mind allowing you to feel better, function better, be happier and improve everything in your life. A unique collection of highly effective methods that remove any mental barriers that may have been preventing you from achieving your most cherished aims and ambitions. No qualifications are needed. Whatever nationality, religion, colour, sex, sexuality or football team you support, anyone can use these amazing secrets to feel strong, confident, energised and powerful so the only question left to ask is how much happiness can you actually cope with?

In between these techniques are a series of anecdotes and other information providing explanations of the various modalities involved and why they are so important in today's ever more dystopian world. The contentions here are mainly quite unusual inasmuch as they are inspired by little known modalities that sceptics might wish to hoard away under the heading of woo-woo in dark, secluded dungeons from where they will never again emerge. Indeed, such are the negative influences around us concerning these kind of techniques that some may find it hard to believe that they will help in any way at all. If so I understand how you feel. As it happens many of my regular clients felt exactly the same way on first hearing but they soon discovered that these methods are actually quite magical and have the power to transform your life instantly.

Nevertheless, some may doubt the approach and there was a time when I might have done so myself. So please feel free to take me to task about anything and everything I put forward just like I probably would if the roles were reversed. My email address is book@petergilmour.com if you wish to make contact.

Generally speaking, people are fascinated with these methods, particularly hypnosis, and wherever I go there is an appetite to know more. So I find myself talking about my work all the time both privately and at my various events. Naturally, there are always a few who cast aspersions on the whole premise and that's absolutely fine. I welcome their questions. However, those who seek a positive impetus to their lives yet stubbornly continue thinking and doing whatever it is they are already thinking and doing can be sure not much will change, their ambitions and dreams will remain beyond reach and they will be stuck as fast as super glue. But if those good folks can find a way to step outside of their comfort zone and adopt different strategies then they will, without any doubt, have a much better chance of success. This is the way to kick-start a process of positive change. My work and this book are about helping people rid themselves of negative influences, find the route to happiness and reach those things they feel are just beyond them. Stepping out of your comfort zone is clearly the key to achieving this. With that in mind let's have courage and move forward. They say the mind is like a parachute. Always works best when it's open. Of course you don't have to believe any of this but if you can open your mind to accept that it may be true then you will open the door to wonderful possibilities including a better, happier, more fulfilled life. Promise.

By the way, this is not stuff that popped into my head yesterday. These various techniques, which I harvest from many abundant orchards around the globe, have formed the basis of my work with athletes, business folk, artists, musicians, entertainers, dancers and anyone else who has knocked on my door seeking help with one issue or another for about twenty years. One of my clients calls it Peter's Panacea. During that time I have avidly sought the best and quickest ways to help people in a variety of areas and in particular to be happy, fulfilled, content, inspired etc. I realised long ago that it's a never ending process of researching, discovering and developing new techniques and the more I investigate the more it dawns on me that the best answers, and there are quite a few, are simple, rapid and potent. One conclusion I've reached for certain is that what works best in most cases is a cocktail of different approaches because they have different effects on the brain and one reinforces the other. Herein are some of the same techniques I use every day with clients some of whom pay a small fortune for the privilege but you are getting them for the cost of this book which is a mere £10. By the way, and please feel free to tell all your friends and acquaintances about this, the book makes a wonderful gift for any occasion! Of course you won't have the amazing pleasure of my presence in the room guiding you through the process with my usual wit and charm but hey, what do you expect for a tenner? The exercise that follows is worth a fortune all by itself.

Exercise 1 - Ball Sway for Cross-Hemispheric Balance

For this exercise you will need a ball about the size of a tennis ball or you can use an orange, an apple, a mobile phone, bunch of keys or even a bottle of water. Something you can easily pass from hand to hand.

Stand with your feet slightly apart and take a nice, big deep breath in and out while tapping the third eye point in the middle of your forehead. Now begin to sway round from side to side. Feel yourself beginning to relax. Close your eyes. Now, as you swing from side to side pass the ball or whatever object you're using from hand to hand. Pass it don't throw it but make sure the ball passes across the central line of your body in the middle of your stomach. As you do this, allow all the fear, doubt, worry, anxiety, trauma, any negative feelings and emotions to drift away until you feel quite calm and relaxed. Allow positive feelings and emotions to flood through your mind and body. Normally this takes about two minutes or less. It's all about balancing the left and right hemispheres of the brain. When this is accomplished you feel calm and focussed. What do people do when they pray? They put their hands together. This performs a similar function because what it does is combine the left and right sides of the body's

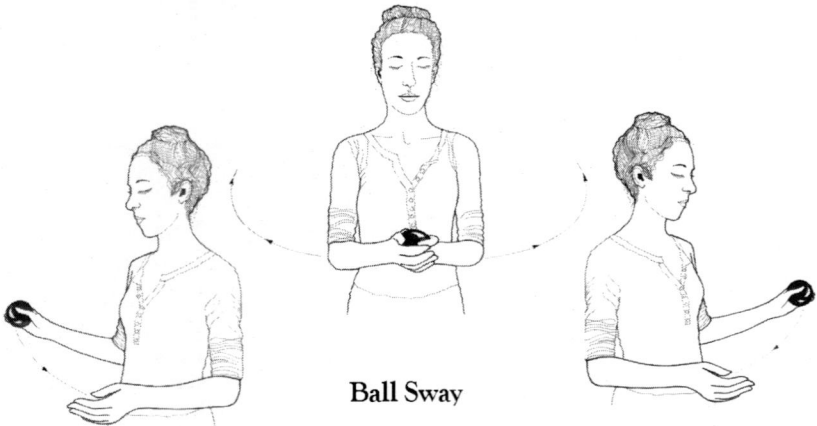

Ball Sway

energy system and this brings about a meditative state. When we sit back in an armchair and stretch out our legs we normally cross them. Same thing. It is the body's inbuilt mechanism for relaxing and we all know instinctively how to do it. The point about this exercise is that it heightens the effects of combining the left and right hemispheric energies and creates a calming, meditative yet energising effect.

To be done first thing in the morning or whenever you need to be relaxed and focussed.

How much happiness can you actually cope with?

'Happiness is the meaning and the purpose of life, the whole aim and end of human existence.' - Aristotle

What do you want in life? This is something I often ask my clients and it usually stops them dead in their tracks because it's not a question they get asked very often. After a short period of mild confusion, some might answer that they want to be successful or rich or famous. But when questioned more closely the undeniable fact which soon emerges, blinking in the light of sharp focus, is that what they really want most of all is to be happy even if they can't quite put a finger on what it means or how to achieve it.

Many have an underlying feeling that something is missing in their lives. But whatever that thing is, they allow the stress, anxiety and pressing 'responsibilities' of modern life to stand in the way of getting it. In fact, there's little doubt that the missing thing, floating so very tantalisingly somewhere out there in the void, close yet disconcertingly invisible, is that rare and valuable commodity called happiness. Happiness trumps all other feelings. Why do some allude to success, money, fame etc? Because they believe those things will make them happy. Happiness is the ultimate feeling or, to quote a recent TV commercial, 'The best feeling available to a human being.' Well, apart from one maybe but that's the subject for a different book!

What would you say? On a scale of one to ten how happy are you? Usually the answer is between five and seven but in twenty years and thousands of clients I can only remember two who have answered with a ten. Maybe you feel that happiness is an abstract concept that might exist sometime in the future. Many people do. So in that respect I have an absolutely crucial message to impart which I fervently hope you'll be willing to take on board. You don't have to believe what I say but if you can accept that it may be true you will open the door to wonderful future possibilities. No, that wasn't the message. This is the message - There's no need to wait, you can be happy right now because by using the very simple yet potent methods described here in this very book for just a few minutes every day you will feel better, function better, be happier and improve every aspect of your life. Yes, it is that simple.

Actually, you don't even have to use all of the methods here, just the ones you like best and feel are best for you. Indeed, it could even be the case that a single method will do the trick all by itself, I've seen it happen, but generally speaking the combination of a few techniques works best.

Go inside and check your happiness level now on a scale of one to ten. This is an easy task. Just follow your instinct and allow your subconscious mind to provide the number. Later you can check it again after doing some of the exercises scattered throughout the pages of the book. In the vast majority of cases stress, anxiety, fear, panic, trauma and other negative feelings start disappearing immediately and are usually completely gone after about five minutes or even less. That doesn't necessarily mean job done but it can do and often does. So make sure you keep up the exercises on a regular basis because they are the recipe for confidence, energy, success and happiness. Legendary American motivational speaker Zig Ziglar said 'People say that motivation doesn't last. Well, neither does bathing. That's why we recommend it daily.' Well the same applies to the exercises herein. Do them regularly for the best effect. Make changes to them if you feel that doing so will suit you better. It's like everything else that you want to do well. The more you practice and experiment the better you get at doing it and the more you learn and grow.

People often ask me how often the exercises should be done but there is no definite rule. The simple equation is that the more you do them the better it is. My best advice is to do them first thing in the morning because you will have a better day and you will feel that you're having a better day. How will you know? It's a feeling you will come to recognise and enjoy. You can also do them at other times of the day. Times very probably when it simply occurs to you that you'd like to do them or maybe when there's an issue to deal with. If you are the sort of person who needs a structured timetable for these things then please do set regular times to do them but don't be surprised if you end up not being someone who needs a regular structured timetable to control your life. There maybe times when you need to prepare yourself for a challenge such as a sporting match, an interview, a business meeting or perhaps even a romantic date. If so then do the exercises beforehand and be relaxed. Feel strong, confident and powerful. Feel yourself performing in a fantastic way and sail through whatever you're doing easily, effortlessly and successfully.

All these exercises can be used to dial down the bad stuff such as negative emotions, fear, doubt, worry, stress, anxiety etc. or dial up the good stuff like confidence, energy, positive feelings and emotions, great performance levels, happiness etc. You can do them as much and as often you like. It is impossible to overdose on these methods so feel free, it's perfectly safe. Nothing bad can happen to you. Only good things happen with these techniques. Amazing things in fact. Promise.

Most people have at least one burning issue and in many cases a number of burning issues affecting their lives adversely but never get round to actually dealing with them either because they don't know how to or because they just accept these kind of difficulties as a normal part of life or because, as they say, life gets in the way. They tend to adopt the 'sweep it under the carpet' strategy which, roughly explained, is really just a cop-out determined by the negative tendencies in their minds. They fall prey to the little voice inside their head which says 'Ignore it and it will probably go away'. They can't be bothered to be bothered about being bothered. This is not a constructive approach because untreated issues are quite likely to build up in your mind and eventually create a huge pile of emotional excrement that becomes even more difficult to shift and this makes you even more unhappy. In extreme cases, as more issues are added to the festering, bubbling mass it builds up into an overwhelming pile of increasingly more volatile excrement that eventually explodes like a faulty pressure cooker and you're left with the messy task of scraping the gooey remains of your troubled mind off the kitchen walls. So why not deal with the issues now or better still, before they arise? Therefore, instead of being dark, depressed and dysfunctional we can switch over to happy mode and enjoy drinking wine and dancing in the fields as we fulfil our wonderful potential as loving, joyful human beings. (I know, blimey!).

How can we do this? I hear you ask. Well, whether your issues are work, relationship, health, emotional or money related, carrying out the exercises set out here is the way to go about draining the murky waters of negativity and sparking the flames of positivity. (How's that for poetry? No answers necessary thank you. Very much. Indeed).

By the way, during the course of this treatise I make quite a few analogies about sport and clearly that is because of my extensive work over the years with athletes, coaches and teams etc. However, it is incredibly important to note that everything here, including all the modalities, methods and techniques which I have slavishly discovered, invented or in some cases nicked in a serious and prolonged study of these matters are relevant to all people in every walk of life whatever they are doing and even, indeed, if they are not doing anything. You do not need to be a world champion to benefit from my advice here. You do not need to be anything at all.

According to academics the only people who don't experience unhappiness are either psychotic or not in the land of the living. Accordingly therefore, if you are unhappy to any degree it means that you are neither mad nor dead so this at least gives us something tangible to work with. You see? Things are getting better already.

Here's what to do to make them even better still: Focus on the issue you wish to deal with, get it right in the front of your mind and measure its intensity on a scale of one to ten. One, not much - ten, quite a lot. Just allow your subconscious mind to suggest the figure and take the first number that comes. Then, concentrate on doing some of the exercises. Start with a breathing exercise then the ball sway, the happy tapping exercise and the nine gamut procedure. The normal result is that you feel the intensity of the issue you're dealing with diminishing almost as soon as you begin and in many cases it disappears straight away. As you go through the exercises, check from time to time on the one to ten scale and notice how it comes down. Sometimes it takes a bit longer, depending on the person and the issue, so go through a few rounds of exercises checking on your level after each exercise. This way you can find out which ones work best for you.

When the issue has gone it inevitably gives rise to another question 'Will it come back?' Often at this point during a session if the client asks me this I might reverse the question and ask if they want me to put it back which is usually greeted with a horrified reaction palms held up in a kind of blocking gesture as if I were a customs official who'd just announced he was about to perform a full body cavity search. I take this as a pretty good indication that the procedure has worked quite well.

By the way, the answer to the question of whether the issue

will return is generally speaking no. Sometimes the effect is rapid and dramatic and at other times more subtle but these methods work for most people most of the time. It depends on the person, the issue and the method being used at any particular time. More often than not, once it's gone, whatever it is, it doesn't come back. Of course life has a way of throwing up surprises, challenges and shocks so even at some time in the future if you do happen to feel something nasty creeping up on you then you can just treat it again very simply and easily but in the majority of cases this isn't necessary. Nevertheless, my heartfelt advice is to pick out some of the exercises and do them regularly by which I mean every day. I teach all my clients these techniques to take away and use themselves so that they always have the tools at their disposal to deal with whatever and whenever issues arise. After all, we're only talking about simple methods that take a few minutes, not a lifetime of intensive therapy. They are the same techniques as right here in this book. Or at least some of them anyway because there are hundreds of such techniques drawn from various modalities and there is only room for a few of my favourites here. So when you finish reading the book you're left with three options if you want to know more. Come to one of my workshops, which I sometimes call play-shops, (or organise one. I'll travel anywhere in the world to talk about my work and demonstrate these techniques), have an individual session with me or wait for the next book. Remember, you don't need to have a negative type of issue to benefit from these methods. As an athlete, business executive, singer, dancer, actor, chef, manager, retail worker, driver, builder, plumber, electrician, nurse, doctor or anything else at all you can use them to enhance positive feelings and emotions such as confidence, belief, focus, happiness etc, in order to achieve your best performance level or just simply feel good, dare I say excellent, about yourself and your life. So whether you have an issue to overcome or wish to enhance your abilities and possibilities, please use these techniques regularly and your life will improve starting now. Promise. The only good reason not to do them is because you don't want your life to improve in any way at all in which case why on earth are you reading this in the first place?

Exercise 2 - 5-Second Eye Movement

I have to tell you that this is simply an amazing technique.

It only takes about half a minute but in that very brief moment of time it can install a new and positive mind-set. Like many of the exercises presented here, it both calms and energises your mind.

Accordingly therefore, think about the issue you want to deal with and rate the intensity of it on a scale of one to ten.

One, not much - ten, a lot.

Sit or stand up straight and keep your head still throughout this exercise.

Close your eyes for five seconds.

Open your eyes.

Look to the left as far as you can for five seconds.

Look to the front for five seconds.

Look to the right as far as you can for five seconds.

Look to the front for five seconds.

Look up as far as you can for five seconds.

Keep looking up and take a nice, big, deep breath.

As you breathe out, lower your eyes slowly down to the ground.

Relax, that's it.

Measure the intensity of the issue and check how far it has gone down.

If necessary do it again.

Do this exercise whenever you feel the need.

Feel better.

You're a What?

'The ultimate source of happiness is within us.' - Dalai Llama

Years ago when I was still green behind the ears I used every opportunity to let people know I was a Hypnotist and had it printed on business cards which, if I do say so myself, looked very smart indeed. Whenever someone asked me what I did I would reply with great enthusiasm 'I'm a Hypnotist' and observe the look of alarm that inevitably spread across their face as they absorbed the information. I could almost hear what they were thinking. Can he read my mind? Is he doing it now? Will he turn me into a chicken? Indeed, just a mention of the word Hypnosis invariably sets bells ringing, pulses racing and hearts fluttering. You almost have to lock all the doors and windows to stop everyone running out of the room. Maybe that's why I like it so much. During the business card period I grew to relish the minor panic induced by that word and truth be told there were situations where I'd invoke it on purpose just to enjoy the effect it created. Whenever I found myself in a place where I met new people, down the pub, in a coffee shop, on holiday, at a football match, in the gym changing room, at a party, anywhere at all really, I waited for that inevitable moment when someone would ask me what I did so I could utter the word Hypnotist, maybe with a slight tinge of menace if I was in a playful mood, then monitor the response. Often either a stunned silence or maybe a comic shielding of the eyes to mimic warding off my evil powers. Some would step back smartly to establish a clear distance between us as if I was Harvey Weinstein inviting them into the shower. Often it drew the hilarious quip 'Better not look into your eyes then'. Ha ha very funny mate. Haven't heard that one before. It was almost as though the very word hypnotist sent them into some kind of mindless trance.

When I handed out my flashy (yet tasteful) business card,

people took a short glance and I can't tell you how many times they reacted by asking 'Ah, hypnosis, does it work?'

I mean really. What kind of answer did they expect? No it's complete rubbish? Load of old nonsense? Don't risk it mate? The correct answer of course is yes it works beautifully well thanks. But in my naivety it took ages to develop such a clear response and let people know that hypnosis is a perfectly safe and effective therapy for most of the conditions we face in modern life. For instance, stress quite simply becomes a thing of the past when you discover hypnosis and all the other amazing techniques we're talking about here.

Hypnosis is a wonderful therapy that, even in its standalone form, helps all kinds of people in all kinds of ways but I have discovered that it is even more effective when combined with other psycho-sensory modalities such as tapping, NLP, Psy-Tap, eye-movement therapy, breathing exercises and others. Together they provide the perfect tools to solve issues such as anxiety, stress, fears, phobias, smoking, weight, pain, confidence, energy, sleep, happiness etc. They are also brilliant if you want to quit an addiction such as cigarettes, cocaine, chocolate, crisps, champagne or anything else beginning with c. Procrastination is another issue easily dealt with by hypnosis but we can talk about that later...........

For anyone wishing to raise their performance level in sport, business, acting, dancing, singing or any other art or discipline these simple yet potent techniques are exactly what you have been looking for. They can help you boost confidence and focus and allow you to enter inspired mental states and perform at the height of your powers in no time at all, guaranteed. Yes, guaranteed. How can I be so sure? Because I see my clients enjoying the positive benefits of these things every day. For many it is life-changing.

So just in case you are in any doubt or feeling cynical about this, let me just state that I am a qualified and experienced

Hypnotist of many years. Not a stage Hypnotist who makes a joke out of it but a clinical and motivational Hypnotist who helps people very quickly with issues that in many cases they can't find a solution to anywhere else such as anxiety, stress, public speaking, IBS, chronic fatigue, depression, smoking, weight etc. Although it is a daily activity for me, I realise Hypnosis is not a familiar subject for everyone so let me assure you that it is an enjoyable, relaxing and inspirational experience. And if you need any further assurance let me also mention that I have worked at fourteen professional football clubs and with a number of top world-class athletes, business leaders, celebrities, and other figures from the world of arts and entertainment (including a number of world champions). Practically all of them were sceptical about it until they experienced the wonderful effects it creates.

In my continuing desire to glean more knowledge about the subject I have sought out many of this planet's most illustrious exponents of the art of hypnosis and other energy medicine modalities, squeezed them for information and amalgamated their collective wisdom with my own methods.

Herewith, I pass on some of that knowledge to you dear reader in order to help you achieve whatever you want to achieve and in the process make a small step towards my childish dream of peace and happiness for the whole world and everyone in it with the possible exception of Jose (grumpy guts) Mourhino. Only kidding! I want him to be happy too.

Terrible Toxins

'My favourite word? It's ACT.' - Ai Weiwei

There are many reasons why people become stressed, anxious, traumatised etc. such as relationships, the way we treat each other, money, health, work, environmental and other matters. But one aspect of our environment affects us all in a very potent way particularly, but not only, if we live in a large conurbation. The aspect to which I refer is that of toxins.

We all constantly ingest toxins of different kinds and they course through our energy systems causing substantial and negative effects to our minds and bodies. When I say toxins I don't just mean traffic fumes. Yes, we know that car exhausts are responsible for a huge amount of pollution and ill health. Years ago it was thought that petrol cars were the worst culprits in this respect emitting carbon dioxide that was rising up through the atmosphere and depleting the ozone layer which was our only protection from the blazing heat and ultra-violet rays of the sun. According to the science of the time diesel vehicles were less harmful and we were heavily encouraged by environmental agencies, politicians and those who cared about the quality of our environment to switch over from petrol to diesel cars. Those of us who were persuaded to do this went around with haughty expressions and holier than thou attitudes particularly when confronted by any of those petrol car driving heathens who clearly didn't care a jot that they were destroying the living environment. We were entitled to be smug. By sacrificing a smoother petrol drive for the much clunkier, chug-chugging, less comfortable and far less cool (in the vernacular) diesel vehicles, we were making a personal sacrifice for the sake of society at large. We were saving the world. We were modern day Tolpuddle martyrs, modern day suffragettes. But lo and behold all you sinners! It was a total load of bollocks! Please excuse the language but sometimes it is necessary. More recently they discovered that it wasn't so much the carbon dioxide from petrol cars but the nitrogen dioxide from diesel cars that was causing all the trouble. Now diesel was the culprit. Now scientists informed us that diesel vehicles of all kinds - cars, lorries and buses were spewing out millions of tiny plastic particulates that were invading the lungs of us defenceless, ordinary folk and making us thoroughly sick. In London alone this was thought to have contributed to the deaths of up to nine thousand people in one year alone. In the New York World Trade Centre atrocity of nine eleven only 2,996 people died. What was that? Did I just say only 2,996? But it is a fact that air pollution in London was responsible in a single year for the deaths of three times the number of people who perished in the worst terrorist atrocity in history. If terrorists were to attack and kill nine thousand people on the streets of London it would pretty much herald the start of world war three.

We'd have tanks on the streets for sure and the government would convene in an underground bunker. I know what you're thinking. Close the door and don't let them out again. (The politicians in the bunker I mean). But seriously, this is an incredible scale of human misery, pain and illness caused entirely by an incompetent government which over the years has allowed such thickly toxic air to develop and to which we have all now become victim. Let me stress again, people are literally dying from this in large numbers.

It's a mystery why we're not all out on the streets demonstrating our disgust about this and if more people knew the facts maybe we would be. By the way, as far as our government's culpability in the matter of people dying is concerned this doesn't even take into account what shady activities our armed forces might be up to around the world or who we sell arms to. This may be a different political story but is nevertheless connected because it is another element of world affairs that makes us fearful and unhappy for ourselves and our kids. Just because deadly military action is happening in another country far away doesn't mean we are not affected by it. And we are.

The government in the UK has stated its intention to get rid of petrol and diesel cars by 2040, that's twenty-one years hence. How many people will die by then? Why don't they act now and save a few lives? Maybe because they don't want to upset the automobile industry which makes and sells the vehicles in question. Car manufacturers employ huge numbers of workers and would lose great piles of money, pay much less in tax and have to invest billions of kahunas if they switched to making electric or hydrogen powered vehicles now. This is quite simply madness. What's it to be, cars or human lives? We need to get rid of all these vehicles now, clean up the air now and enable ourselves to be healthier and happier now. To live now. Not in twenty-one years' time. No wonder we're all stressed out. No wonder we all need the therapies here in this book.

My Father always used to say 'The world's gone mad.' Now I go around saying it myself.

But it isn't just the pollution from vehicles that affects us. We now know that the main polluter worldwide is concrete, the material used to build practically every modern building everywhere. The main ingredient of concrete is cement which is one of the prime producers of carbon dioxide, a potent greenhouse gas. The manufacturing process of other, everyday items such as paints, varnishes, furnishing fabrics, carpets, water, clothes, food etc. is such that they're chemically treated and also emit harmful toxins that we all ingest. On a sunny day when rays of sunlight shine through our windows we see a myriad of little particles floating around in the beams. This is pollution. A clear manifestation of the toxins in question. They enter our bodies and create effects that not only cause conditions like asthma and other chest infections but also clog up and block our bodies' energy systems. In order to feel good and function well our energies needs to be flowing freely and effortlessly around the body. When our energy is blocked or flowing slowly or backwards we feel sluggish and tired. As if our batteries are in backwards. This condition is called polarity reversal or PR. It is not a derogatory term or something to be embarrassed about, it happens to all of us frequently.

These toxins attack us from various directions that people don't always notice or realise. For instance, in the case of insomnia, a debilitating condition suffered by many, an obvious cause is often missed. While we talk about bedroom hygiene such as keeping things calm and turning off electronic gadgets etc. we can forget that the last thing most people do before retiring to bed is to brush their teeth. The average toothpaste is full of chemicals which can be extremely toxic, more so for some than others, therefore our last act before getting into bed is to sabotage our chance of getting a decent night's rest by taking a huge slug of sleep-destroying toxins. I know, you're wondering how to keep your teeth clean and shiny without toothpaste. But the solution is to find a non-toxic toothpaste and they do exist if you look around. One example is turmeric toothpaste which many have started to use. Alternatively, it is a fairly simple matter to make your own toothpaste by mixing ingredients like coconut oil and baking soda. Details for obtaining or making non-toxic toothpaste are easily found online. If you are a sleep deprived person then please give non-toxic toothpaste a whirl and you may very well be pleasantly surprised albeit I do not suggest it is the solution in every case.

Toxins are present in all areas of our lives. The air, water, food, soaps and other toiletries, make-up etc. etc. Therefore, the equation is very simple. The more we can resist them the better we feel. Much of the therapy I propose in these pages is designed to resist the effect of toxins and get our energy systems flowing. The good news is that there are many simple exercises we can use to counteract toxins and the PR effect so that we feel good and happy and full of energy.

Here's a tapping exercise that is specifically designed to resist the effect of toxins and get energy flowing. Everything works better after happy tapping so it's an excellent idea to put this exercise first or second in your routine because the others will work better after it. All my clients love and enjoy this exercise. They like doing it and they like the effect it has. It is designed to ward off the worst excesses of toxin intake. If you don't know about tapping there is an explanation later in the book but in the meantime please bear with me because although you may think it a bit daft to start with, as I did, you will eventually realise that tapping is actually quite magical, as I did. I recommend the following exercise to be done at least once every day first thing in the morning and if you do, I promise you'll have a better day. It is also well worth returning to it a further couple of times during the day when you feel you need a boost.

Very often people burst out laughing after doing this exercise and if not laughing they at least end up with big smiles on their faces. It is a wonderful example of a simple technique that has a big effect much like all the exercises in the book. Enjoy.

Exercise 3 - Happy Tapping

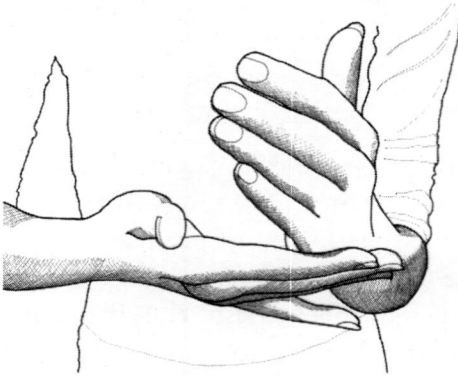

Karate Point

Think about what you want in life. For many people it is happiness and the wording I use here reflects that. But you can alter the wording. For instance, you may want to use the word healthy or confident or focussed or loved etc. instead and adjust the text as you go through it.

Read through the exercise and all will make sense. Tap on the karate point (point you would use to execute a karate chop) on the side of one hand about twenty times while saying out loud:

I want to be happy (or inspired, successful, healthy etc.)

I can be happy

I will be happy

I am happy

I'm okay.

Tap on your upper lip under the nose about 20 times.

Tap under your bottom lip in the crease of the chin 20 times.

Tap on the karate point on other hand while saying out loud:

I want to be even happier

I can be even happier

I will be even happier

I am even happier

I'm okay

I'm more than okay

The Wall Man

'It's your world and you can change it.' - Malala Yousafzai

A very famous hypnotist once told me I was the wall man. We were having lunch at my expense at a posh hotel in London because I wanted to learn a particular technique from him and at one point he said 'Peter mate, you help athletes and business folk and others break through those mental barriers and achieve great things.'

'Yes.' I agreed.

'You help them smash through that wall that's holding them back.'

'Yes I do.'

'Well that's it then.'

'Is it?'

'Yes.'

'What?'

'You're the wall man.'

'Am I?'

'Yes, you prat. The man that helps them break through the fucking wall.' I sensed he was becoming impatient with me. Now this guy had quite a large following of devoted acolytes for whom he was a mentor of sorts but, much as I respected his great abilities as a Hypnotist, I wasn't looking for the kind of guidance a mentor might bestow. Anyway, I have my own acolytes who hang on my every word thank you very much. But he was insistent and wouldn't let up. 'Get some business cards printed up and call yourself the wall man. They'll be queuing up at your front door.'

'Okay I will.'

To be perfectly honest I had never been short of clients even though I'd never advertised my services. Clients just somehow found their way to me. But on reflection I thought the wall man business seemed like a fairly good idea and I began to visualise myself on TV being questioned by our finest inquisitors on the country's most popular current affairs shows.

'So Mr Gilmour, you're The Wall Man and at the UN summit conference you managed to persuade all world leaders to enter a treaty abolishing weapons of war and entering a legally binding agreement of peace and happiness supervised by the Dalai Llama.'

'Yes Jeremy.'

So I got the cards printed up and started handing them out all over the place but just about every person I gave them to, including some well-known athletes and business folk, took one look at the card and reacted in exactly the same way.

'The Wall Man? What's that then?' Time after time the same bloody question. After a while I was thoroughly fed up with constantly having to explain what the hell it meant to almost everyone I gave the damn card to. I mean okay, maybe athletes are not necessarily the most erudite of folk but what on earth did they think the Wall Man could mean? That I was a bricklayer or something?

Need an extension to your house? Call the Wall Man.

So just for the record let me just state quite clearly and unequivocally that I am a highly experienced and extremely effective Hypnotist who loves his work and has taken the trouble to study the subject very deeply and also to learn a dozen or so other very potent modalities and even invent a few special techniques of my own that augment and strengthen the effect. Altogether this works incredibly well for my clients who derive great benefit from it. By the way, some of those clients are quite high achievers in various fields. My purpose in writing this now is so that you too can derive the same benefit from these methods as they do. You too, dear reader, now have access to some of the amazing secrets

I have discovered over the years and can begin to utilise them immediately to improve your life in whatever way you want or need and be happier. Because we all need to be happier. Unless we have just won the lottery or had a baby or our football team has won 5-0 or we are basking in the after-glow of amazing sex we all need to be happier. I know it might sometimes be hard to find the happiness we seek in today's harsh and dysfunctional world but that's the paradox we are dealing with because the happier we are the easier and more pleasant and less dysfunctional life becomes. It is a vicious cycle that must be broken and of course those who continue to make it difficult will eventually be run out of town. Life is not supposed to be difficult. It's supposed to be easy and joyful. Right on brothers and sisters! Power to the people!

Of course, hypnosis just on its own is the most wonderful therapy that can and does help people in many ways such as getting rid of stress, anxiety, fears, phobias, panic, stopping smoking, losing weight (or gaining it), pain relief, confidence boosting etc. etc. It's an excellent tool for removing addictions such as cigarettes, cocaine, chocolate, crisps, champagne or anything else beginning with c. Indeed, even if you have no issues at all, hypnosis will lift you into an area of amazing expectation and fulfilment that you never knew existed. For anyone wishing to raise their performance level in sport, business, acting, dancing, singing or any other art, discipline or profession I can assure them that hypnosis is what you need particularly when combined with any of the various other modalities I practice.

Furthermore, I am quite prepared to come and demonstrate this for you if you want to invite me. This applies to sports clubs, businesses, schools, universities, charities or any group of folks who wish to stimulate their minds or raise their performance levels or function at the height of their powers or all of the forgoing.

I teach all my clients self-hypnosis and encourage everyone I come across, whether they are my clients or not, to learn and use it on a daily basis to improve every area of their lives. The simple fact is (and simple facts are the best kind) that when you close your eyes and go inside, whether it is meditation, prayer, daydreaming or hypnosis, there is only one place to go. That sacred place inside. The place where all change is possible. So whilst hypnosis is similar in some ways to meditation it is much more direct and focussed and certainly a whole lot easier. I say this because many people tell me they experience difficulties with meditation. If that is the case for you then hypnosis will provide an excellent alternative.

There are full instructions of how to carry out self-hypnosis in the following pages and if you need any further information please feel free to contact me directly at book@petergilmour.com.

Lashings of Milk and Honey

'You will not be free until we are free.' - Desmond Tutu

Who do you feel sorry for first? In a cruel and violent world where war, famine, pestilence, corruption and greed are rife we sometimes struggle to work out who is most deserving of our sympathy. The starving Mothers of Africa whose breasts are too withered to feed their babies, the refugees of Syria whose entire world has been bombed to smithereens, the flood victims of Bangladesh who watch helplessly as their whole world just floats away from time to time, the innocent children of impoverished countries who gulp down diseased, foul water because it's very hot and they're very thirsty and it's all there is to drink, the poor Rehingya women who were tied to trees and repeatedly raped or the countless tortured slaves around the world forced to toil endlessly with no joy or reward, no rights, no hope, no life at all really.

In such a world it's almost churlish for those of us who live in the comfortable western world to consider such a fanciful concept as our own happiness.

Given the most fortunate accident of birth that allows us to enjoy pleasant lands of moderate climate, lashings of milk and honey and relative peace, we should be happy.

Thankfully immersed in aesthetically pleasing aspects of culture which excite our senses, there is absolutely no reason not to be happy. But generally speaking, we're not.

Perversely, we tend to equate happiness with money and material possessions (or in the younger demographic with being on television, having the latest phone or sleeping with a premiership footballer) and yet we know deep down that these things are not the answer. Indeed, the unhappiest people I've ever met have been the richest whilst the happiest belong to the very poorest in India. People who have hardly anything at all if you don't count shining eyes, a beaming smile and a serene countenance. Of course, as we wander around aimlessly in our confusion we make feeble attempts to salve a troubled conscience by asking how we could possibly allow ourselves to wallow in our own happiness when there's so much suffering in the world. But the simple fact is, and again we all know it, that the most active tenet influencing our comfy existence is that of 'out of sight out of mind'. So even though the harrowing evidence of man's inhumanity to man is beamed nightly via TV into our living rooms in glorious, full-colour, enhanced cinemascope we have a mental switch that either turns it off or converts it into an adventure movie. Indeed, we indulge in so much glossy, violent drama that it becomes increasingly difficult to differentiate between reality and fantasy. As we relax in the evening over dinner, we can quite easily watch news reports of psychotic terrorists shooting, raping and chopping innocent peoples' heads off while deciding what to have for pudding or who to vote for in The X Factor.

If you tell me you have a toothache I can sympathise but I can't feel it. We can't feel it but they can. They're quietly weeping tears of unbearable pain because there's simply no escape. And the more they shift position to try and alleviate the pain the more it hurts. Even more pain on top of the already unbearable pain. Searing pain right through the heart.

My work and the various methods and techniques I encourage people to learn and use are the exact opposite of this terrible pain and everything associated with it. The antithesis of all the raging violence, injustice, unfairness, fascism and iniquity that abound in the world. (And rubbish, reality TV as well for that matter).

We may or may not be able to change the world but we can certainly influence our own corner of it. The happier we are and the more love we have for ourselves and each other the more that love and happiness will spread out and envelop those around us and then it's up to them. Completely naïve for sure but it's my contribution to a better, happier world and if we all work together and believe in what we are doing I am totally convinced we can create a positive difference. In this I am in good company because just about every significant philosopher agrees that the only thing of any real value in our existence is love.

Roger Bannister - The Four-Minute Mile Barrier

Author's note: *As I edit this chapter on 4th March 2018, the radio murmuring softly in the background breaks the sad news that the legend Roger Bannister has just died. God rest him.*

On 6th May 1954 British athlete Roger Bannister stepped out onto the Iffley Road running track in Oxford in an attempt to break the world record for the mile which had stood at an incredibly stubborn 4.01.4 for nine long years. During that time, many great athletes had tried and failed to break this daunting standard to the point where it was generally considered to be beyond the capability of any human being. Indeed, scientific opinion of the time warned that if you were foolhardy enough to attempt such a feat your heart might explode in the process. Thus it became known as the four-minute mile barrier. But Bannister and others, particularly his great rival the Australian John Landy, had other ideas. They were convinced it was viable to run a mile in under four minutes and each was determined to be the first to do so.

On that day in Oxford Bannister made history as he fell exhausted through the finishing tape in a new record time of 3.59.4. It may only have been a mere a split second faster than four minutes but it re-defined what was possible and as news of the achievement spread slowly around the globe it was generally hailed as one of the finest moments ever in the world of athletics. Bannister instantly assumed his place in history and became a household name. The Iffley Road track was promptly renamed the Roger Bannister running track and many years later Bannister was honoured at the opening ceremony of the 2012 Olympics in London.

Curiously however, in the twelve months following Bannister's record breaking moment, quite a number of other athletes managed to run the mile in under four minutes the first being John Landy who broke Bannister's momentous record by a full second only about a month after it was set. So after nine years during which it was considered impossible now everyone was doing it! I exaggerate of course, not everybody, but these days, many athletes are capable of running the mile in under four minutes and by 2017 around 5,000 had been recorded as having done so. What does this tell us?

It's all about belief. Bannister had such intense belief in his ability to break the four-minute mile barrier that he was able to overwhelm scientific opinion of the time and make the impossible possible. But it was only after he'd achieved it that others believed they could too.

The moral of the story, like so many of the most wonderful things in this life, is very simple. If you believe you can do something there's a chance you will do it. If you don't believe you can do it you probably won't. So my advice to ambitious folk who wish to achieve great things, is to practice believing. This book contains the secrets of exactly how to do this. It contains many methods, techniques, sessions, tricks and triggers designed precisely to help you work towards the Bannister model of unconquerable belief.

By the way, the mile is no longer run as a competitive distance but the last record set was by Hicham el Guerrouj in Rome in 1999 and stands at 3.43.13, more than a quarter of a minute faster than the so-called impossible time achieved by Bannister. Clearly, the four-minute mile barrier was merely just a mental barrier. We need to smash through these mental barriers if we want to make something of ourselves. And that's in life generally by the way, not just sport.

Aloha (the breath of life)

'A significant difference between a living person and a dead person is that the living person is breathing.' - Peter Gilmour

We must talk about breathing. When I mention breathing exercises to clients and groups I can tell they are not as excited as if I mention Hypnosis or NLP or Eye Movement Therapy or any of those other psycho-sensory type things that sound a lot more interesting and sexy than silly old breathing. So let's get it straight folks, breathing exercises are an incredibly important ingredient of the very tasty recipe I advocate here and absolutely fundamental to the whole shebang. You can change your life using breathing exercises alone even if you don't use any other techniques. But having said that, please make sure you do use the other techniques because they make everything much better.

Right now though I want to recommend the great benefits of breathing exercises which are very brilliant and not at all boring.

Consider this. We can live for three weeks without food. We can live for three days without water. But we can only live for three minutes without breathing. The big difference between someone who is alive and someone who is dead is that the person who is alive is breathing. We breathe on average around twenty-three thousand times a day. That's quite a lot. Knowing this, it is easy to conclude that how we perform this basic function makes a big difference to our lives. It does. You can also conclude that if you make small changes to your breathing patterns you can make big changes to your life. You can.

We all have certain pressures to deal with and these pressures can make you tense. When you're tense your muscles tighten automatically and you need strategies to prevent it happening. When you feel uncomfortable it affects your performance in whatever activity you are involved because your mind overloads and shuts down. One method you can use to relieve this situation is a breathing exercise. There are hundreds of them. My 3,2,1 breathing exercise, which follows this chapter, has proved immensely popular across the board and many have thanked me for teaching it to them. When I say teach, it's not something you need a PHD to comprehend. It is a two-minute exercise and absolutely anyone can learn it in no time at all and then they can benefit from it for the rest of their lives. It is about the simplest exercise possible but please don't be fooled. The effect is marvellous. Before I describe it for you, here's a simple pre-exercise that demonstrates the effectiveness of breathing. Like I say, it's a demonstration and not intended as a therapy albeit it pretty much acts like one. I often do this with groups in workshops and they are always amazed by it.

Make every muscle in your body tight. Squeeze everything up as tight as you can. Head, neck, torso, arms, legs, buttocks, fingers, toes, everything. Go on, no one's watching.

Now while you hold all those muscles tight as you can, tight I said, take a nice, big deep breath and hold it in for the count of three. Now exhale very slowly. What do you feel? What happens to your muscles? They automatically relax right down don't they? This is a simple yet very powerful demonstration of the power of breathing and how breathing affects the muscles. It is relevant whatever your walk of life. However, athletes in particular, being so wrapped up in the physical realm, should easily be able to understand by doing this how breathing affects the muscles and how doing regular breathing exercises will enhance your performance level.

As I have already said and now say again for emphasis, abdominal or diaphragm breathing (belly breathing in the US) is a basic and very important technique and usually the first thing I teach any client who's not already aware of it because it is quite simply fundamental to wellbeing. Indeed, I'll do breathing exercises with clients even if they are already well aware of them. Here's an example of what I mean. It is the perfect example of a simple technique that makes a big difference to feelings, emotions and performances whatever your walk of life and the way you feel generally.

Much of sports psychology concerns adjustments to the athletic arousal level but the same applies in business or any other walk of life. What it refers to is the emotional state of the athlete, artist, entertainer, barrister, business person etc. while they are in the flow of performing their respective professions and activities. Competing, negotiating, performing, presenting, the flow of creation etc. Whatever you do during the time you are doing it. The point is to manipulate the emotional state until the optimum level is reached, neither over nor under cooked. This is achieved very easily and quickly with breathing exercises, NLP, TFT, Hypnosis or whichever combination of the methods in these pages suits you best.

There is an established psychological school of thought maintaining that two deep breaths held for three seconds creates the optimum arousal level. As you may have noticed I rarely go along with established schools of thought but in this case I do. We can use breathing techniques for a range of purposes easily and effectively. The point is to manipulate your physiology and the following exercise is perfect for this. I have added a simple visualisation to a basic breathing pattern and the result is a brief yet potent technique which pretty much everyone finds incredibly useful.

I cannot tell you the number of people who have thanked me profusely for teaching them this very simple technique and anyone who has attended my events and workshops will be familiar with it because it is one of the things I make sure to include every time. As I have already said and make no apology for saying again, just this exercise on its own can change your life (but still do the others to make it even better).

This exercise forms part of my pre-match routine for athletes or pre-meeting process for executives or pre-performance technique for musicians, singers, dancers, comedians, entertainers etc. but it also forms part of just about every treatment with anyone whatever the issue or circumstances. I suggest making it part of your daily exercise routine and using it every morning. You can use this exercise before any challenge you may face such as exams, work interviews, performances, speeches, difficult meetings and negotiations. Any situation where you need to centre yourself. It is a centering exercise. Accordingly therefore:

Exercise 4 - 3, 2, 1 Breathing

Take a nice, big deep breath, right down into your abdomen so it pushes your belly out. Hold it for three seconds. While holding your breath say to yourself three, two, one, relax.

As you breathe out slowly feel all stress, anxiety, fear, doubt, worry and all the things you don't want flowing away from you. You can see it all flowing out into the atmosphere. All negative emotions and feelings flowing out and away. Leaving you feeling strong, confident and powerful and ready for the next challenge.

Remember, breathe in relaxation and calmness, breathe out all stress, anxiety and negative emotions. Relaxed but ready is the motto here.

Feel good?

Relaxed but ready?

Great.

Do it again.

Neck-top Computers and the Magic Ingredient

'How wonderful it is that nobody need wait a single moment before starting to improve the world.' - Anne Frank

When clients turn up for their first session it's often a last resort having exhausted all the possibilities formal medicine has to offer. In many cases it is also after experimenting with a retinue of strange practices they have discovered on the internet offering tickets on the slow train to Nirvana for a small fortune. Somewhere along the line they've been told they have depression or stress or trauma or anxiety and haven't found anything to make it go away.

'I've tried everything.' They say.

'You haven't tried this.' I reply.

Then, before they've even taken a seat they tend to say something like 'I know it's going to be a long haul.' Because that's what they have been led to believe by people who really should know better. 'Oh really' I ask 'who said that?' They speak with a kind of tacit acceptance that their issue is going to be difficult to fix and that they were smart enough to have realised this before I told them. But what I actually do tell them is the exact opposite. That they've been brainwashed into thinking in this negative way and of course saying it just compounds the issue. Because energy psychology (the vague category to which my methods belong) in all its myriad, mystical forms is a supersonic combination of treatments compared to anything else available and many of these debilitating, ostensibly incurable conditions can be successfully treated in minutes rather than years using these wonderful methods. It is much better to tell people their condition can be treated quickly and get them believing it will be gone soon because if that's what they believe then that's what is likely to happen and naturally also, vice versa. Surely this is not such an outrageous idea. These days many people accept that if you adopt a positive attitude towards fighting an illness you can recover more quickly. The question that perplexes them in many cases is how exactly to adopt this positive attitude. If they read this whole book they will know. So will you.

Having said that, I hasten to add that not all conditions can be treated in five minutes and if people turn up with very deep emotional trauma they may very well need extended care and attention. But the vast majority are not like that at all. They have merely fallen foul of the ubiquitous difficulties and complications that continually arise in a dysfunctional and often hostile world which have caused their mental state to deteriorate so that they are low on confidence and self-esteem. It happens to even the most capable and competent of folk. Such as the CEO of an international company who cowers in his office, frightened to death by the scale of responsibility his job entails. Or the single mother frantic with worry and tiredness as she juggles the time constraints of a full time job with the child care needs of her sensitive son. The brain is a fantastically complicated piece of kit, more powerful than any computer they say, but we aren't issued with a service manual for when this neck-top computer of ours breaks down which means that when problems occur we become unhappy and confused because we don't know how to fix it. Sometimes with all the pressures of life and under severe stress the brain can quite simply make a mistake but with the right tools we can fix it easily and effortlessly.

However, far from helping as they are supposed to, medical professionals tend to exacerbate this kind of situation because they are not at all clear what to do and will either prescribe drugs or refer to Psychiatrists who enter the scene clad in their Armani finery and laden with even stronger pills and potions which they scatter in all directions thus turning the patient into a quivering zombie and holding up any chance of a real recovery in the foreseeable future. This is why they warn the patient it will be a long haul. Because their methods clog up the system and close out the cure. People will probably recover anyway in the long run so whether there's a cure or not is open to doubt.

Actually, when treating people it isn't always necessary to even know what the issue is because by carrying out certain exercises in what is known as a content free format, that's carrying out the exercises without focussing on a particular issue, the issue resolves itself. How? Because the unconscious mind knows what needs fixing and once you stimulate its attention it will direct positive energy towards the most pressing issue. Trust in your unconscious mind and everything will be okay. I may have said this before in the previous pages and will most probably say it again in the following ones because it is an incredibly important point. This is not psychotherapy folks. Not the paid friend business. Now is always the time to start and get the damn thing fixed. Unless you absolutely insist on hanging on to those nasty, horrible feelings for a bit longer of course.

The purpose of this book is to pass on these simple, rapid, potent techniques to as many people as possible so that they will have the means to solve their own issues and therefore to create a happier, healthier, more peaceful and loving world. It is also a companion to the Happiness workshops I run around the UK and abroad throughout the year. At these popular events I demonstrate how to be happy now or with certain sport, business or performer type audiences how to be inspired now. They are not lectures but humorous, vibrant, interactive workshops including interesting anecdotes, videos, demonstrations and group hypnosis. They represent a light-hearted way of introducing innovative methods drawn from cultures far and wide that instantly transform your mental state and improve your life in what is becoming an increasingly baffling and stressful world. A unique opportunity for anyone to learn at least ten simple, potent techniques you can use every day to feel better, function better, be happier and improve every aspect of your life. Great fun indeed.

I say ten but I don't mean **the** ten. It's the first ten that come to mind or that feel relevant to any particular audience because I have a massive resource of these amazing secrets drawn over the years from a variety of sources and cultures throughout the world. Anyway, it's often more than ten depending on or how much time we have on any occasion and how long anyone allows me to prattle on. These methods are all entirely holistic and natural and safe and exist freely in nature for everyone to utilise. You don't have to use all of them, just the ones you like best and feel are best for you. The more you use them the better you feel and eventually you reach a point when the only question left to consider is how much happiness you can actually cope with!

In these pages I set out some of my favourite methods. Here also there were supposed to be a total of ten but my passion and enthusiasm drove me to include a bonus of an extra few much to the chagrin of my publisher who wishes to publish a second volume sometime in the future. Actually, there are about twice that number in the book but the publisher needn't worry because there are hundreds of them. Plenty more for a second, third and fourth volume and after that maybe we'll have such a happy world that I won't need to bother any more!

Please let me have your thoughts and reactions because I'm always keen to know how this stuff is helping people and how I can improve it. You don't have to believe what I'm saying but if you can open your mind to the fact that it may be true then you open the door to a new and exciting life full of happiness and fulfilment and I really do feel I can guarantee that.

To all the athletes, business folk, professionals of any type or description and those involved in the world of arts and entertainment out there, if I said there was an entirely safe and legal way of instantly transforming your performance level beyond anything you imagined was possible would you be interested? Of course you would. Well stand by because this is it! This is the winning edge. The zone for athletes, the groove for musicians and the flow for anyone else. This is the thing you always wanted but didn't know how to get. The magic ingredient that allows you to feel great and perform at your best. To function at the height of your powers. To achieve your wildest dreams. To fulfil your true potential. This is it. Right here. Now. Truth be told, you don't even need to be a professional in any of the categories mentioned above or have any qualifications at all to benefit from the information in these pages because the same is true whatever your walk of life. Driver, baker, nurse, builder, retail worker, plumber, factory worker, electrician, farmer, computer programmer, cleaner. Whatever you do, wherever you live, whatever your race, nationality, religion, sex or sexuality or even, dare I say it, football team, the price of the book is exactly the same as it is for everyone else. The very best paid footballers, pop singers, film stars and government ministers etc. Furthermore, the information in it is exactly the same and you, whomever you are, can achieve the same quantum leap in your confidence, energy, success and happiness as everyone else by reading, absorbing and using the exercises herein. It's easy. We are all brothers and sisters and we are all equal. The more we love each other the happier we will be. Promise.

Exercise 5 - Energy Spin Out

Think of an issue you want to deal with and locate in which part of the body you feel it.

As a rough rule of thumb if it's in the stomach it's fear, in the chest, anxiety and in the head it's trauma. In some cases people feel it spreading over from one area to another, usually the stomach and chest and it's easy to make a conclusion about what this means. But it is just an indication which I have found helpful rather than conclusive in the scientific sense.

Focus in on the issue and notice what colour it is.

Now notice the shape.

Now imagine taking the issue out and holding it in front of you. Spin it clockwise. Make it spin very fast. Faster, faster. While it's spinning change it to the opposite colour. If it's black make it white. If it's green make it red etc. etc. keep it spinning, faster, faster. Now spin it the other way. Faster, faster, faster. Change the shape. If it's round make it square. If it's a triangle make it oval etc. keep it spinning round for a minute or so. No need to be exact.

Now stop the spinning, put it back inside and see how you feel.

Better yes? Good.

Do it again and feel even better.

Sex and Laughter

'Love is wise, hatred is stupid.' - Bertrand Russell

It wasn't the Ritz but it was the swankiest establishment in those provincial parts and a good night's sleep was my principle ambition. I was there to deliver a motivational workshop and had travelled the night before to avoid a ridiculously early start in the morning when my own motivation might have needed a great deal of encouragement. After the long journey from London, a nightcap before turning in was an appealing prospect so I found the lounge and was sitting at the bar ruminating quietly when my attention was drawn to the guy sitting next to me who was knocking back drink after drink in such rapid succession that he was seemingly speeding headlong down the fast road into oblivion. I observed his behaviour out of the corner of my eye and began to feel quite worried about him. I mean what on earth could have happened?

What could have induced such destructive behaviour?

Eventually my instincts clicked in and I asked him 'Are you alright mate?'

He turned slowly in my direction.

'Well' he said 'I shouldn't really be doing this with what I've got.'

I felt a shudder.

'Oh dear, what have you got?' I asked and braced myself for the reply.

'About two pounds fifty.' He answered.

'Oh dear.'

Now there are three things we can learn from this little story. First, it can be unwise to jump to conclusions about people because we all do it and we are very often wrong. Second, if the guy really had some terrible disease as you might have been led to believe, what course of action should he have been taking? Weeping into his soup in uncontrollable grief or filling up whatever time he had left with love, laughter and alcohol and having a great time?

Whatever he wanted as far as I'm concerned.

Oh yes, and third by the way, it's funny. Did you laugh? Are you laughing? When I tell this little tale or one of my other carefully selected anecdotes to a workshop group they usually laugh their heads off and it's often the first thing I do because I have a carefully selected collection of tried and tested, very funny stories and my workshops and events are about happiness and laughing is the body language of happy people. You cannot laugh too much and although you often hear people say they nearly died laughing I am not aware of any case where this has actually happened. In fact, laughing is probably about the safest and most enjoyable activity available to us apart maybe from having sex and if you can laugh while you are having sex then you have probably achieved the ultimate success albeit your partner may not appreciate it much.

Very sadly indeed my friends, the state of modern society is such that we don't have anywhere near enough sex and we don't laugh anywhere near enough whether we are having sex or not. No wonder there are so many grumpy folks around the place. I know it can be hard sometimes but I'm trying to make it easier for everyone because life is not supposed to be difficult.

I've had a word with him upstairs and he agrees. He told me it's not the point at all in fact it is the antithesis of the point. He is adamant. (How could he be anything else?) And in case you're wondering, yes he is a bloke and yes he does have a large beard and yes heaven is in the sky above just out of sight of living people and yes there are angels lying about on the clouds all around him and red-faced little cherubs with little willies flitting here and there playing trumpets, watching TV and eating chocolates and yes he's looking down on us all 24/7 so he sees everything you do even when you're on the toilet so you'd better watch out if you have any pretensions about wanting to end up in his place upstairs because he simply will not stand for any nonsense and yes he is eternal and yes he can do anything, and yes he does know how to fire thunderbolts at those who misbehave. So now you know and there's no need to worry about it anymore as long as you behave yourself. Don't say you haven't been told mate. I just told you.

I do this work to help people be happy and love each other as much as possible and there is no shortage of customers because so many are stuck in negative emotions.

The moral here is that life is incredibly precious and we should make as much of it as we possibly can. Enjoy every single moment. There are plenty of methods, techniques and modalities in these pages to help you do just that so there's really no excuse.

Eat, drink and be merry folks for tomorrow you may die!

Incidentally, there's another story about a chap who had been burning the candle at both ends and goes to the doctor complaining of feeling tired. The doctor examines him and reaches a conclusion.

'It's a case of too much wine, women and song I'm afraid.'

The patient is shocked. 'What can I do?' He asks.

'Well you must give up the wine and women immediately' says the doctor 'but you can sing as much as you like'.

Now then, are you laughing or do I have to come over there and tickle your belly?

Woo Woo - Knock Yourself Out

'Confidence works wonders sometimes.' - Roger Federer

So just to recap in case you forget, here's the good news. There are many simple, rapid, potent exercises which, if you do them every day, will make you feel better, function better, be happier, be more confident and improve everything in your life. Yes! You have my personal, unequivocal guarantee about this. I'm not saying you have to use all of them, just the ones you feel work best for you. Although it is also true that the methods that may seem less effective in the beginning eventually become more effective later in the process. Some of these amazing exercises are right here in these pages and that is what this book is all about. To pass these techniques on to you together with a few explanations, anecdotes and down home philosophy to convince you to use them every day and improve your life beyond anything you might imagine. Why? Because I'm trying to make the world a happier place. Naive I know but I can't help it. But this is just the tip of the iceberg because there's a resource of hundreds of these wonderful, very powerful techniques from a massive range of modalities so reading this is just the very beginning of the story, not the end.

For the purposes of this book and for your convenience I have cherry-picked a cross-section of some of my favourite methods and even some I invented myself. Do them in the morning if you can, five minutes is all you need because then you'll be able to look forward to a great day. Do them at other times of the day too when you get the chance and see how everything in your life improves. You can spare five minutes can't you? Excellent. Make the decision now. Now is always the time. Incidentally, you think you might have read this before don't you? Maybe it's déjà vu. Well no actually. Whilst I quite realise that repeating things is a cardinal sin in writing I do it on purpose so please don't be surprised if I repeat myself during the course of these chapters like I did in the last few paragraphs because I want to make absolutely sure I get the main points across and that you are in no doubt at all that if you do the things I suggest, and they are not difficult, you will enter a new chapter of happiness and fulfilment in your life. There, I've said it again. Also, by the way, the unconscious mind loves repetition and that's where your behaviour patterns are created so the more I say it the more your unconscious mind hears it, believes it and registers it's true. Trust in your unconscious mind and everything will be okay. More about this later.

Exercise 6 - Mental Delete Key

'When I think back on all the crap I learned in high school it's a wonder I can think at all. And though my lack of education hasn't hurt me none I can read the writing on the wall.' - Paul Simon

The more I do this work the more I realise that the answers to the biggest questions in life are very simple. We tend to carry around the bitterness, regret and trauma caused by experiences we had earlier in life. The school-kid who is told they are no good at a particular subject and as a result loses interest in it altogether. School-kids who are actively discouraged from following subjects in which they are passionately interested because they are told it's not viable or not suitable as a vocation. I'm talking particularly here about music, sport and the arts. A young tennis player I once helped was told by his county tennis association (that's the guys who are supposed to be creating interest in the game amongst kids) that he had no hand/eye coordination and banned him from the county squads he was desperate to join up with. Many are given this kind of advice at an early age such as a girl I knew who was told at the age of twelve she was not artistic and eventually became an internationally renowned sculptor. The tennis playing lad could have given up when he was told he had no chance but, encouraged by his dad, he continued independently without help from the national body LTA, rose consistently in the rankings and eventually became the number two 16u player in the entire UK and an international player in GB teams. His career was cut short by injury otherwise he would almost certainly have become a professional player which is incredibly difficult to do. What is the matter with these people who shatter the dreams of young people with their nonsensical ideas? Reach for the stars is my advice to young people who dream of doing things. Or anyone else for that matter.

We all tend to beat ourselves up about things that go wrong and can't seem to avoid those feelings of self-recrimination. That we made a mistake, that we are to blame for something, that something is our fault. There's a persistent little voice in our minds telling us we are idiots, that we are not good enough, that it will never work, that we can't do it. In sport people make a mistake and can't get it out of their minds. For instance, a tennis player plays the wrong shot and loses a point as a result of a momentary lapse and then beats him or herself up about it ad infinitum. 'Stupid.' They say to themselves. 'You idiot.' 'You're useless.' Etc. etc. Maybe a lot worse than that too. Point after point. Set after set. They just can't get it out of their minds. Johnny Wilkinson, the iconic, England rugby player who scored the winning free kick in the world cup final in 2003, talked about the little voice in his mind that said 'I can't do it'. To him I say change that voice to one that says 'I can do it'. But sport is just an example, it happens in all walks of life. Musicians who play a wrong note, dancers who miss a step, singers who forget the words, business people who make the wrong investment. Even those who mistakenly utter something embarrassing and wish the earth would open up and swallow them whole. They all should know that the past is no good to us anymore. Close the door and leave it there. The only thing that matters is what you do now.

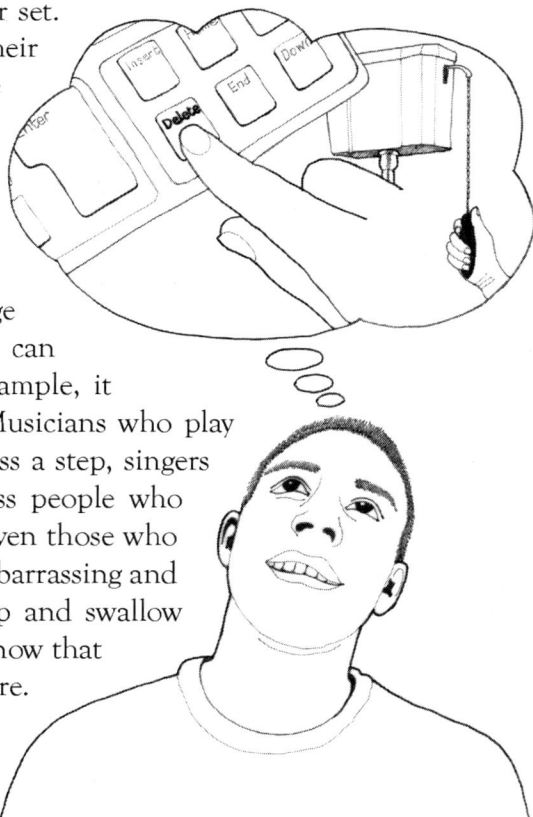

Time to resist and fight back against these limiting beliefs so the voice in our minds says 'I can do it!' This is how we do it. As with all the methods here it is very simple. The more we learn, the more we realise that the answers to the most difficult issues are very simple. Think of the issue, the mistake you made. The little voice that says you are an idiot or similar. Get it in the front of your mind. Visualise the computer keyboard of your mind. Focus on the keyboard, zoom in on the delete key and press the delete key. Feel the issue disappear from your mind. That's it. Gone. Alternatively: Think of the issue. Visualise the toilet of your mind. Zoom in on the handle. Pull the chain and flush the issue down the toilet. Send it to the seaside. See it go, bye, bye. Feel that the issue has gone. That's it too. Gone. Change that little voice in your mind to one that says 'I can do it'.

Mad Uncle Harry

'I am angry. We should all be angry. Anger has a long history of bring about positive change.' - Chimamanda Ngozi Adiche

I'm often reminded of things my mad uncle Harry used to tell me when I was a mere slip of a lad many years ago. I say mad because that's how we all thought of him but in fact he was a Psychiatrist and quite a respected one at that with a number of books and papers to his name. However, I often wondered what it would be like to be a fly on the wall at one of his therapy sessions and if you'd be able to work out who was the therapist and who the patient. He had a lively mind for sure and not many could keep up with him. That's probably why they said he was mad rather than admitting they couldn't understand what he was on about. I always felt he and I had a bond of some sort. Maybe something to do with a shared disdain for the status quo. He held strong views on all matters of the day which he took every opportunity to expound but his fast talk, wild eyes and habitual switching of the subject sometimes made it difficult to understand where he was coming from and even more difficult to get a word in edgeways. When I once confessed that I didn't believe in what he was saying about one of his particular contentions, religion, he threw up his arms in a typical gesture of impatience and bellowed loudly 'Don't believe in it?' Despite his scientific approach he was a devout Jew. It never ceases to surprise me how many scientists are passionately religious when religion is about as unscientific a concept as you can get. The sudden power of his voice shook me to the bone and I was just about recovering from the shock when he suddenly roared again even louder 'DON'T BELIEVE IN IT?!!!!' He could see I was startled and that was probably his intention. To imitate God and frighten me out of my wits. (Told you he was mad.) He was a child psychologist don't forget. Well he succeeded because on this occasion I was shaking in my boots. On and on he went in his bellicose, agitated manner 'If you went to the zoo and looked at an elephant would you say you don't believe in it?' He yelled.

For him everything was as totally obvious as that in his mind. Big as an elephant and a big elephant at that. Maybe what he meant was what we now refer to as the elephant in the room. Perhaps that was the kind of idea in his mind but this was the early sixties and long before any such concept had loomed in anyone's imagination let alone entered into the lexicon of everyday expression. Looking back, mad uncle Harry was probably miles ahead of his time and maybe not as completely potty as his reputation.

These days I tend to be a bit like him myself inasmuch as unashamedly stating my fairly radical opinions whenever I get the chance. In gym changing rooms, doctors' waiting rooms, coffee shops, at dinner parties, at home etc. much to the great disdain of many of those listening (particularly at home!) and I get the impression from time to time that they think I'm potty too. For instance, I'm always talking about my work and the kind of therapies put forward in this book and at times I can clearly sense the unconscious sniggering. I'm afraid some people just can't help themselves because their lifelong conditioning determines they will have long ago filed my kind of stuff away under the category of woo-woo in their minds. Not fit for human consideration. But it is often they who raise the subject partly because they think it's good for a laugh but partly also because I think they are secretly fascinated by the subject matter, particularly hypnosis, and while they might try to prove me wrong they perhaps subconsciously want me to prove it's true. Hypnosis is a subject that most people find fascinating and deep down they want to know more about it, even maybe want to believe in it but although they show a bit of interest it's obvious they don't want to let the mask slip and accept what I say in front of their friends because then they'll be the potty ones too. They have issues like we all do and maybe I suspect secretly hanker for me to treat them with my voodoo but they certainly wouldn't want anyone else to know. Why would I say this? Because on a number of occasions I have been contacted for a session the day after a social event by an unlikely customer who had seemed uninterested over dinner and now goes to great lengths to stress that nobody else should know about it. They don't need to say that because all treatments are carried out in strict confidentiality anyway and I would never discuss anything about a client without their permission. No therapist would. People like to have a controversial character to stoke the fire of debate and amuse their friends. Look at my bohemian friend the hypnotist who comes to dinner. I fall for it every time because it's a chance to tell the story and maybe influence someone to cross the floor and join the good guys. My own little revolution carried right to the heart of the establishment. I always had a burning desire to change the world for the better and suppose I always will. But I'm not always sure who is really listening. For many the subject of my work is a bit of a novelty but to me it's my whole world. Go on, say it. This guy is paranoid. Yet if only I can persuade them to trust me a little more because with every day that passes I gather more and more evidence of the absolute truth of the case I'm making and the excellent benefits of these amazing psycho-sensory techniques in helping all kinds of folks in all kinds of ways. Beware, if you invite me round I will take the opportunity to spread the word even though I know some people find it hard to take on board at first hearing (or second or third or fourth for that matter).

Indeed, in the case of tapping for instance, I had the same reaction myself when I first heard about it as I have explained elsewhere in this treatise. What? Tapping on different parts of your body can change your mental state? Don't be daft. Of course that was a long time ago and long before therapists were using it as much and as successfully as they do today. Yet despite the veritable Mont-Blanc of proof concerning the efficacy of tapping and other psycho-sensory techniques there is incredible cynicism about it and those propounding such methods are thought of as quacks. To those cynics who think I'm potty I say you don't have to take it from me. Just have a look around the internet and you'll find a wealth of information about the great success of therapists the world over using hypnosis, NLP, tapping techniques and many other types of energy medicine. These techniques help people stop smoking, lose weight, cure fears, phobias and habits, relieve pain, reduce stress, anxiety and trauma, increase confidence and happiness and many other issues too. In the area of addictions, they can very quickly help you get rid of dependence on cigarettes, cocaine, chocolate, champagne, crisps and anything else beginning with c. (I might have already mentioned this). But it's not scientific say the cynics, there's no empirical evidence to prove it works. It's just a placebo etc. etc. Oh really? Well did you know that Einstein used hypnosis when he discovered the law of relativity? And that he used hypnosis regularly to hone his thinking? And that he once said 'There is only energy.' That's pretty bloody scientific in my book.

And suppose it is just a placebo? So what? Why on earth does that matter at all as long as it helps people overcome the severe, debilitating problems that affect their lives so adversely? Recent research has shown that people react positively to placebos even if they are actually told they are taking a placebo. If it works, use it. That's what I say my friends.

Magical Underpants

'*Sport has the power to change the world. It has the power to unite in a way that little else does. It speaks to youth in a language they understand. Sport can create hope where once there was only despair. It is more powerful than governments in breaking down racial barriers. It laughs in the face of all types of discrimination.' Nelson Mandela*

Over the years I have worked with quite a number of professional athletes particularly footballers, tennis players, cricketers and golfers helping them to enhance performance levels and get rid of negative tendencies. When I first meet them, most don't have the foggiest idea about even the most fundamental ways of preparing their minds for competition and they regard my methods with great suspicion. During their careers, quite a few have developed certain lucky rituals such as wearing the same outfit on match days or having the same pre-match meal, or putting their left sock on first or listening to a particular music track or saying a prayer or crossing themselves or bowing towards Mecca or looking upwards, presumably to God, with their arms outstretched. When I ask them what mental preparation they use before or during matches these are the sort of things they talk about. Indeed, these kind of methods seem to be utilized, accepted and even encouraged quite widely throughout the world of top sport even though there is absolutely no scientific basis for doing them. Let's be clear, these rituals are pure superstition and have absolutely no connection to scientifically devised mental training exercises. I always say that if you think it helps then by all means do it and I stand by that but please don't place this frippery in the same category as the motivational techniques I coach because it is an entirely different thing and will not have anything like the same potent effect by any means at all. Not even close mate. The problem with these antics is that they are a vague appeal to some kind of all-powerful outside deity or unknown force to intercede and boost your powers in some mystical fashion whereas what you really need is that pure energy and unshakeable belief that come from within. The truth of the matter is that everything you could possibly want to know is inside you. Yet despite the fact that I can provide a perfectly decent track record plus perfectly cogent scientific explanations for my methods, it is my approach that draws doubt and scepticism and which I am continually called upon to justify despite the fact that it is the product of many years of avid study, research and experimentation and has been well proven at all levels of sport for, in my own case, over twenty years. Meanwhile those athletes who wear their favourite underpants on match day in the belief it will somehow improve their performances are encouraged to indulge in their quasi-religious dabbling as if it were a divine right. This is because most coaches haven't got a clue about the mental realm and are unable to provide advice on the subject. Many sports coaches languish in the mistaken belief that you are either born with mental strength or will never have it which is of course a brazen cop out. Therefore, they are quite relieved when athletes come up with an idea off their own back even if it is some kind of medieval fertility rite. Again I say, if you think it helps then be my guest. But please don't confuse it with properly devised and proven mental training methods because it is not by any means at all the same thing. Got it? Good.

At every football club I've worked at, the performance level, measured by results after I arrive compared to results before, shows that there has generally been an improvement of about fifty percent in terms of points and undoubtedly more in terms of confidence and general feelings of well-being amongst players and staff. But if you quietly mentioned to a sports psychologist over dinner that a such a performance improvement of fifty percent was pretty much instantly possible they would probably double over and collapse in the soup. Why? Because they seek a modest improvement of one or two percent as a result of around a year's work and would regard my claims as fanciful nonsense. Sadly, it is they themselves who are more wracked with limiting beliefs than their unknowing client athletes because throughout their academic training they have been conditioned to accept a very meagre norm and dismiss the kind of results my methods achieve as quite simply impossible. What a great shame. I refer you to the story about Roger Bannister elsewhere in this tome which illustrates the weakness of this negative kind of mind-set. These guys transfer their own limiting attitude to their subjects who in turn are unable to progress further because they are now programmed to reject ideas of great success except in some foggy, distant long-term scenario. This is obviously the exact opposite of what is supposed to happen. I am convinced that certain sports psychologists resist raising the bar too high in case doing so invites failure. British athletes rarely say they want to be the world number one. When I first work with an athlete, say a tennis player, I ask them about their ambitions and almost without exception they say they want to reach the world top hundred. If I then suggest that maybe they could have a go for world top fifty they are stunned into silence and after a moment or two of deep reflection come up with the old chestnut 'Well you have to be realistic'. What idiot feeds them with such rubbish? Someone does because I have heard the same thing so often. How I hate that word realistic. It expresses an element of doubt and itself promotes limiting beliefs. It might even be the most negative word in the English language. They say it because it has been drummed into them by people who should know better. I very much doubt if Roger Federer or Rafa Nadal or Ronaldo or Michael Jordan or Tiger Woods or even our own Lewis Hamilton or Andy Murray ever said they wanted to be the fiftieth best in the world or that their ambition was anything less than to be the undisputed world number one. My advice to those rather timid young folk who are striving for their unrealistic target of being number fifty is to have courage, believe in yourself and reach for the stars!

In every case when I have started work at a football club it has been at a point where the team has been losing matches, usually three or four in a row and in one case seven. In all of these cases the team has played well and won in the first match after my involvement began. Would that have been the case if I hadn't had a session or two with the players? Don't know. After each of those first matches I overheard sentiments in the changing room such as 'Well we were due a win.' Or referring to me 'Maybe it's just a coincidence.' Not the slightest suggestion it might be anything to do with the effectiveness of my work with them. I am pleased to report however that my continued involvement always brings about a much better appreciation of my methods as performances and results improve as they always do. Perhaps they are right and it is all just a coincidence but if that is that case there are quite a lot of them because the outcomes form a similar pattern every time and not just in football but every other sport and in every other walk of life.

Exercise 7 - The 9-Gamut Process

Tapping sequence to remove anxiety and negative emotions (9 gamut process). This is the classic tapping procedure common to all the tapping modalities. Total magic. Promise.

Use once or twice a day for as long as necessary whenever you feel the need. Think about what makes you anxious, stressed, frightened, worried and rate the intensity of the feeling on a scale of one to ten. One, not much - ten, a lot. When looking in your mind for the appropriate number just take the first one that occurs to you. The first number that pops up. No need to spend time searching. Tap about ten times each on collarbone, under eye, collarbone again, under arm about four inches below armpit and collarbone again. Now tap the third eye spot, collarbone, side of the eye, collarbone again and re-check the level of anxiety which will almost certainly have decreased and possibly by quite a lot. Tap continuously on the back of your hand on the spot between the knuckles of the little and ring fingers about an inch in from the knuckle. (Check the 'gamut spot' diagram on page 60 if you're not sure). Continue tapping whilst carrying out the following instructions. Close your eyes then open your eyes. Keep your head still and look down to one side and then down to the other side. Roll your eyes around one way. Roll them round the other way. Hum a few seconds of a tune such as 'Happy Birthday or 'Jingle Bells' or any other tune you prefer. Count out loud from one up to five. Hum a few seconds of a tune again. Tap about ten times each on collarbone, under eye, collarbone again, under arm about six inches below armpit and collarbone again. Tap on the third eye point, side of the eye then collarbone again.

Stop and check the level of anxiety on a scale of one to ten. This should now have decreased and possibly have disappeared completely. If not do it again and feel it taking more effect each time. The nine-gamut process, as it is known, works for most of the people most of the time. It sometimes works perfectly straight away and sometimes needs a few rounds of the tapping procedure. It can depend on the person and the issue. It always works to one degree or another but the results can be stunning and very often even life-changing.

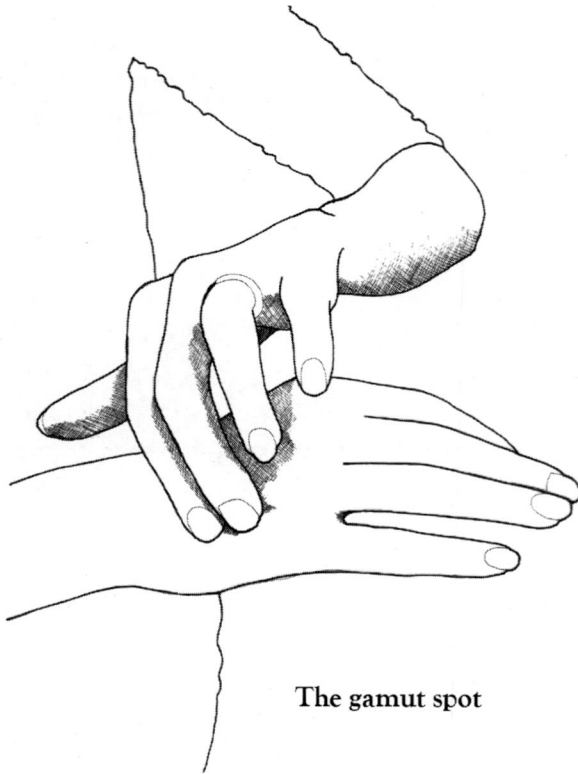

The gamut spot

Quality Quackery

'It's kind of fun to do the impossible.' - Walt Disney

The great Richard Bandler, co-founder of NLP and widely respected luminary in the world of mental engineering, once had the idea to market a product in America called placebo tablets. They had no active ingredient but the claim was that they cured anything. He was forced by the authorities to withdraw them on the basis that it could not be proved they would work. The more likely reason for banning them was that they threatened the market in anti-depressants which adds countless millions in every world currency to the profits of pharmaceutical companies who are an incredibly powerful bunch of guys to fool around with. You can't upset them and hope to get away with it. That's another reason people are doubtful about complementary therapies. Because they have been made to believe that doctors with white coats and stethoscopes are the only people who are able to correctly diagnose and treat conditions and of course the widely accepted main form of treatment is with the drugs they prescribe. Doctors are completely tied to the pharmaceutical industry which funds their very comfortable lifestyles and as such ignore, reject, sideline and pour scorn on holistic methods despite clear proof of their efficacy.

So you see my friends, the evidence is there for all to see. All those who want to see it that is. As clear as the nose on your face. As big as the biggest elephant that ever trod on your foot. And yet despite the huge and substantial body of evidence in favour of hypnosis and other complementary therapies many are unable to see the wood for the trees because to a very large extent these methods are regarded as quackery. Many of those who eventually find the long and winding road to my consulting room are desperate and do so as a last resort having tried everything else including, in many cases, a bunch of real and actual quackery. Of course, the majority never make it because their inherent prejudices are so great they avoid these things like the plague. What on earth is the matter with everyone? Don't they want to feel better, happier, healthier? Couldn't they just humour me a little and tap a few places where I direct them just to see if anything happens? After all, if it's useless they have nothing to lose and everything to gain. The moral here is that you really should be more discerning about your taste in quackery. Or maybe that I should start seeking a cure for the plague!

The struggling NHS in the UK could help itself enormously by enlisting the large bank of local complementary therapists many of whom would gleefully assist in the health of the nation if anyone bothered to ask them. But, as of now, most holistic therapists are completely shut out from applying their expertise in the organisation except in the case of the increasingly ubiquitous condition named after a description of its symptoms, the very popular yet hated, annoying yet treatable, embarrassing yet widespread, uncomfortable and awkward. Yes ladies and gentlemen, boys and girls I give you the one and only, the inimitable, the ever-so-easily-treatable - irritable bowel syndrome !! Or IBS as it is affectionately known. Having the curious distinction of being the only condition allowed to be treated on the NHS with Hypnotherapy!!!! Although God knows why it's the only one because there are many conditions that Hypnosis and other psycho-sensory techniques can treat better than the NHS (or any formal medicine) can such as stress, anxiety, insomnia (taking your anxiety to bed with you), depression, worry, chronic fatigue syndrome (ME), FybroMYalgia, (deliberate capitals) addictions, habits, fears, phobias, pain etc. And furthermore, with energy psychology methods these can all be treated safely, reliably and in double quick time. There's a crisis in mental health the world over and many of those dedicated UK professionals who know how to and are willing and able to help solve it are frozen out of the process. Never mind the poor souls actually suffering from debilitating mental issues, it is those organisations and agencies who are supposed to be helping them who are completely mad.

Tennis Trials

'We are the change we seek.' - Barack Obama

People often ask me how I became interested in Hypnosis and all these other methods and the answer is that my initial motivation was to help my son Josh who was a talented tennis player with great ambition in the game. He was a county champion and amongst the best prospects in the country but what held him back was a foul temper that would erupt regularly for the slightest of reasons (or no reason at all) causing him to play far beneath his normal level and forfeit any chance of winning. An unexpected bounce, unlucky net cord, noises off court, any little thing at all would get him going and then I'd have to listen to him shouting his head off all day and losing matches he could easily have won if he'd just been able to stay calm and focussed. To be fair, it wasn't just him and amongst his peers he wasn't the worst in this respect. All the other talented kids lost their rag too when things went against them because they were all desperate to win and at that very young age they simply couldn't handle the emotional roller-coaster of competition. This type of situation is familiar to many tennis parents and when talking to parent groups I always observe nods of recognition around the room when mentioning it. The rules forbid anyone to talk to the kids while they are playing so it's hard to devise a way to deal with it. None of the coaches I spoke to at the time had the slightest glimmer of a solution so I went looking for one and took it right to the top level of the sport but even the LTA's Head Performance Coach at the time had no answer to the problem and I realised I was on my own. (The LTA is the Lawn Tennis Association, the governing body of tennis in the UK).

It's funny how you find things when you are not looking for them. A chance visit to Ross-on-Wye library produced the first inklings of the solution I was seeking. I had gone there to collect a book I'd ordered but, loving books as I do, when I see loads of them all lined up like that I simply cannot resist a browse and so it was on this fateful day that I was magically drawn to the sports psychology section where a book on sports hypnosis winked at me seductively from the shelves. I could almost hear it saying 'Come on big boy. I've been waiting for you'. At the time of course I had no idea that reaching out for that sexy little book would be the first step in the process of creating a whole new career for myself but as I sat in the library leafing through those pages I was completely drawn in and became consumed by the subject of hypnosis. I realised it contained the answers I was seeking. In the end it took over everything.

So Josh was by no means the only one with this limiting behaviour pattern and to this day it's an ongoing issue. Of course, Josh's great passion was and still is tennis but this story is relevant to kids who play any sport or who have any other talents and passions such as singing, acting, writing, drawing, science, fashion, cooking, knitting, botany etc. Anything at all in other words.

The Book I found in Ross library was Sports Hypnosis by Donald R. Liggett. It represented the first chink of light in a long investigation that continues to this day even after twenty years and I am happy to accept that it is a never-ending quest. A few elementary techniques drawn from this book and others I found on the subject were all it took to adjust Josh's behaviour and allow him to play with a smile on his face, express his talent and enjoy the game more. I was amazed at the effect and the experience encouraged me to study Hypnosis formerly. Now, many years on, I'm a Master Hypnotist and leading Mental Performance Coach with as much experience as anyone of working with athletes up to International level. Furthermore, as a former tennis dad, coach of junior football teams and Chairman and Manager of a semi-pro football club with about ten junior teams, I've experienced the full gamut of vagaries influencing junior and grass roots sport thereby giving me a comprehensive and hard won understanding of the processes involved. Josh by the way is now a highly successful tennis coach with a magnificent CV containing the names of many celebrated world figures.

Dyslexia Dreams

'I used to be dyslexic but I'm KO now.' - Unattributed

In the case of my daughter, Shelley, she was diagnosed with dyslexia in the last year of primary school which we now know was the reason we struggled with tearful reading sessions every night at bedtime. This was over twenty years ago and people didn't know anywhere near as much about dyslexia as they do now. Shelley had managed to maintain a decent level at school despite the reading problems so her teachers didn't notice anything in particular was wrong. But we certainly did and because Shelley's mother was very academic and good at languages and I was an avid reader, journalist and author it was quite a shock for us discover that Shelley had such an issue.

Because the school had no answers or advice we decided to get Shelley tested privately and organised an assessment at the Dyslexia Association in Sutton Coldfield. She called me at work on the car phone as she and her Mother left to drive home from the appointment. 'We're on the way back from Cutton Soldfield.' She said. Bingo! It was the kind of thing she said all the time along with asking us how to spell relatively simple words. How come it took us all so long to realise she was struggling and how come the school hadn't picked it up? But like I said, people didn't know much about this kind of thing then even though about ten percent of school pupils are dyslexic. Teachers don't have time for much individual attention and it's easier to assume that kids with reading problems are just a bit thick when in fact many of those with dyslexia are very bright indeed and achieve amazing success in their lives such as Richard Branson for instance. Yes, the prat who owns the airline, the train company, the phone company, the gym company, the record company, the money lending company etc. Turns out he's a dyslexic prat. Imagine what the dyslexic prat might have been capable of if he could read properly.

There are a number of ways to help dyslexics read easier such as placing coloured plastic sheets over pages and certain strategies of remembering words or parts of words but I had another idea. So I began working with Shelley mainly using hypnosis and interesting things began to happen. Now, many years later I would not say she is entirely free of every semblance of this very annoying condition but I can report that she completed university with a first-class, honours degree and was immediately head-hunted to work in America where she has successfully climbed the managerial ladder of one of the world's largest hotel chains and enjoyed a great career ever since. Would she have achieved the same success without the hypnosis? Maybe, maybe not, I don't know. She is a highly motivated, very bright and ambitious person anyway (which might have something to do with the hypnosis sessions we had even before the discovery of her dyslexia). But that's the nature of this most benign beast (hypnosis). In some cases results are rapid and dramatic and in others they are more subtle. One thing I can say unequivocally and without any hesitation at all is that hypnosis, in common with all the psycho-sensory methods I use, works very well indeed for most of the people, most of the time. Shelley made a success of things due to her own drive, skill and intelligence and I helped her a little in the same way as any other parent, teacher or coach would. I certainly do not claim that I am responsible for her success because she did that by herself. What I do say is that anyone with dyslexia can be helped in the same way as Shelley was and any student or ambitious person will achieve more by utilising the mental tools we all have at our disposal and that includes using the methods I suggest here.

Exercise 8 - Control Room of the Mind and the Big Red Button

I call this the control room because it is a tried and tested method I have used very successfully over the years and the vast majority of my clients have found it incredibly useful but it's had a makeover and is now an all singing, all dancing iPad! We didn't have the iPad when I first used this but there are similar methods around in the wacky world of hypnosis.

It is a very effective technique when used in the waking state but of course it is a thousand times more effective in a light hypnotic trance. So ideally you can use the self-hypnosis method elsewhere in this book and combine it with this exercise. When you reach the point where you are nice and relaxed after going round the body easing up the muscle groups and then counting down as instructed in the self-hypnosis chapter, you then bring in this control room technique instead of any affirmations. Otherwise, you can call me to do it on skype or come round and I'll show you.

Just a brief aside here. Recently a client came from New York to see me in London. He flew for about sixteen hours there and back, plus all the getting to and from airports, immigration, security, duty free etc. Spent four hours with me in the best hotel near the airport where he'd booked a suite, bought dinner for both of us in the same building and then flew back. Altogether he enjoyed a sum total of just under nine hours in the vicinity of Heathrow on that trip and a sum total of over twenty hours getting there and back. God knows what it cost him because he flew first-class and he paid me a pretty decent fee but he said it was worth it. Amongst other things we did on that day was the control room. It was the star turn of the session and he loved it.

The control room works like this. I'm going to give you two versions and you can choose which you like best.

Imagine the control room of your mind in whatever way you wish. Some see old-fashioned dials, levers and switches whilst others see hi-tec computers, screens, flashing lights etc. By now you probably already have an idea of what your control room looks like.

Pick an issue to work on say improving confidence but it could be anything. Energy, focus, belief, motivation, happiness etc. Sit or lie down quietly, close your eyes and drift into a relaxed state. Now in your imagination picture a large door in front of you. This is the door to the control room of your mind. As you open the door you see inside the room and notice that it's full of controls such as switches, buttons, levers and dials (or computers, screens, hi-tec etc). These are the controls that regulate your mind and body. These controls can change everything that happens to your mind and body. The way you see, feel, hear, think and behave. And your desire to raise your confidence levels. Straight away you notice a dial that controls your levels of stress and relaxation. It is labelled from one up to ten. Ten being the most stressed and one being the most relaxed. But the dial seems to be set too high so in your imagination you reach out and turn it down and down and down. Right down to number one. And as you turn the dial down you immediately notice yourself becoming even calmer and more relaxed. Your stress level going down and down and down. And now as the dial reaches the lowest setting you feel totally relaxed and calm and entirely free from stress. You feel so much calmer and relaxed than before. You feel fantastic. And now your mind focuses directly on the confidence control which is also labelled from one up to ten and also seems to have slipped down below the top level. In your imagination you reach out and turn it up and up and up. Right up to number ten. And as you turn the dial up you immediately notice yourself filling up with confidence. And as the dial clicks on to the highest setting you feel a surge of purpose and strength flooding through your mind and body filling you with amazing energy and strong, confident, powerful feelings of success.

You feel your muscles revitalised and re-energised. You feel strong as an ox, fast as a cheetah, as graceful as a gazelle, as powerful as a lion. You feel absolutely full of confidence. You feel a determined sense of drive and purpose lighting you up from within. Creating a positive energy that spins through every part of you. Feel the energy, feel the power as your mind and body click into perfect harmony switching your confidence up to the maximum level and allowing you achieve all your aims easily and effortlessly. Now, with all controls set to maximum performance level and firmly locked in place you turn to leave the room feeling right on top of your game. Fully prepared for whatever challenges come your way. You lock the door with a key and you put the key in your pocket because only you have access to the control room of your mind. You can access your control room at any time even in the waking state to adjust the levels of anything in your life.

The second version which I tend to use more these days is an iPad instead of a control room and icons representing the various issues. In your imagination the icons open up on the screen with sliding controls to adjust the intensity of the issue. Dial up the good stuff, dial down the bad stuff.

But here is the piece de resistance which is my unique and magical hot button which you can take with you when you leave the control room and use anywhere you like. You can keep the button anywhere, in a pocket, up your sleeve or even on your head, and it will activate the control room and return all the controls to the optimum settings just with a touch. So if you imagine activating your confidence to the highest level just a touch of the hot button will zoom it straight upwards and you will feel your energy bristling as your confidence instantly goes through the roof.

You can use your imagination when using this potent tool. A young tennis player I work with sees a massive red button about the same size as she is right next to her when she plays and if she needs a boost of anything at all she just imagines punching the button as hard as she can and feels herself filling up with confidence, energy, motivation, focus, skill. Anything she needs. Needless to say she loves it.

Install it in your unconscious mind and you can use it anytime too and achieve your wildest dreams.

Century of Centuries

'The real professionals step up and say I'm here' - Pep Guardiola

I worked with the great Sachin Tendulkar a few hours before he scored his one hundredth international century. A huge milestone in his career and in the history of cricket and certainly in the lives of every Indian cricket lover which, if you know anything about it at all, includes every single one of the entire population of India numbering one point three billion souls.

For those who are unfamiliar with cricket or this particular story let me tell you that Sachin Tendulkar was a great Indian cricketer and one of the best batsmen who ever lived. Many say the best. He is quite simply a god in India where cricketers are worshipped above all others and Sachin is worshipped above all other cricketers. At the point our lives crossed he had scored ninety-nine international centuries (a century is one hundred runs) and had been stuck on that figure for over a year during which, however much he strived and however much his fans willed him on, he just couldn't get the hundredth. Nobody else had even come close to getting a hundred international hundreds the closest being the seventy-two scored by Ricky Ponting, another great player and former captain of Australia who had already retired from international cricket and would therefore not be improving on his tally. Time after time Sachin went in to bat with the whole of India breathing down his neck. Millions peering intensely at their TVs, poised and waiting on tenterhooks, willing, urging and praying for their great hero to score this hundredth century which would be bound to spark off waves of wild celebrations around the whole country. Every time Sachin took to the crease in a test match in any of the various far flung corners of the old British empire which are the only places where the exquisite game of cricket is taken seriously the cameras zoomed right in and focussed closely from all directions on this highly talented player, diminutive in stature and yet a giant in the history of the sport and the country held its collective breath. Would this be it? Is this the moment? Can he do it? On a few occasions he came tantalisingly close. In a test match in Australia he scored ninety-five but somehow he just couldn't seem able reach the magical milestone and some even began to doubt he ever would. After all, he was approaching thirty-five years old now and no one can play at the top level forever can they?

For Sachin it had clearly become a mental issue that becme more and more unsolvable as the weeks and months rolled on and the innings came and went without success. And then he called me. He was in Bangladesh playing for India in the Asia Cup which is between India, Pakistan, Sri Lanka and Bangladesh. The day Sachin called me India were about to play Bangladesh. He was in his hotel room in Dhaka and I was in Marks and Spencer in Hampstead. Can you help me? He asked. Sure I replied. And so we had a twenty-minute session during which I hypnotised him over skype, energised his mind and a few hours later the little master (as he is known) was scoring his one hundredth international century after not being able to do so for about a year and a half. Cue wild celebrations in Mumbai, Delhi, Calcutta, Punjab, Kochi, Southall and Beaconsfield. Would he have got it anyway? Don't know. 'It was only against Bangladesh.' Some said, as if to suggest Sachin would probably have made a big score anyway because Bangladesh were not considered a particularly good team at the top level and would probably not have been able to prevent the great man's achievement. But in all honesty that's hardly a watertight case because he had played against them many times during the period when he couldn't get his 100th century without achieving it. And anyway, in the event Bangladesh actually beat India in the historical Match in which Sachin got his great century. So maybe they are not that bad after all.

Exercise 9 - Modelling

Be the person you always wanted to be

If you model your behaviour on a person you admire then you can take on all their positive aspects and use them for yourself. As an athlete of any kind, if you model your behaviour on a champion player who fills you with admiration you can step into their body, feel what they feel, see what they see, hear what they hear, perform like they perform, copy their style and success, generally be like them and lift your level to theirs. The principle is exactly the same for those in business, performing arts, teaching, driving, designing, building, cooking - absolutely anything. Pick the person you admire the most in whatever field they are active and follow these instructions.

Close your eyes and imagine standing behind the person you admire. Close your eyes, take a nice, big deep breath and relax. Count from one to three and on the count of three step inside the body of the person you admire. Using your imagination, now you can feel what it is like to be them. See what they see, hear what they hear, feel what they feel. Feel them as they begin to perform their sport, art, ability, talent and move with them. Move how they do. Perform how they perform. As an illustration, let's imagine it is Roger Federer. Feel yourself out on the tennis court, maybe the centre court at Wimbledon. Feel the warm sun on your body, the breeze brushing your face, smell the newly mown grass, feel the racquet in your hand. See your opponent hit the ball towards you over the net. Step in to strike the ball just like Roger does. Forehand, backhand, volley, serve. Feel the certainty, the confidence, the grace and style of this fantastic player and feel yourself playing just like him. Feel all the feelings he feels inside. Now take a serve. Inside Roger's body you serve just like Roger does. Fantastic serve! Ace!

In all the modelling sessions I've ever done with young footballers in the UK, the one player they all seem to admire above all others is David Beckham. Yes that's right, not Messi or Ronaldo or Suarez or Hazard or Couthino or anyone else playing now. The one they all want to be like, well about ninety percent of them anyway, is Becks. Maybe it's because of everything else he represents too. Being married to a pop star/fashion designer, incredibly rich, having loads of successful business ventures, being an international celebrity and a generally cool sort of guy. Heaven knows, I'm beginning to fall for him myself! Seriously though, and I'm talking about kids in academies now, the modelling session is always amazingly powerful and motivational. They love it. But it's not limited to kids. If you do it, whoever and whatever age you are, you'll love it and its great benefits too and you'll get the chance to be like David Beckham or Stanley Mathews (who?) or Roger Federer, or Maria Sharapova or Serena Williams or Richard Branson or Frank Sinatra or Tiger Woods or Michael Jordan or Lady Gaga or anyone else at all who you admire. So for instance if you're a tennis player and you mentally model and rehearse the Federer forehand and the Nishikori backhand and the Raonic serve and the Djokovic belief system over and over during a light, hypnotic trance, then the next person you play had better watch out!

If you're in business and you model the attributes of Richard Branson (favourite of the male section amongst business folk doing this technique) then the next person you negotiate with had better watch out!

See what I'm getting at?

Clever Trousers

'Insanity is doing the same thing over and over again and expecting a different result.' - Albert Einstein

We are creating an environment that is hostile to ourselves. In the UK we have one of the strongest economies in the western world which they say is out-performing various competing economies and yet despite this ostensible affluence all of our most essential services are hopelessly underfunded and the word is that this will get worse. (By the way, just for the record, I am not in competition with anyone but our leaders seem to think we are in competition with everyone else).

So the government claims the economy is flourishing and yet there isn't enough money to fund even the minimum level of wellbeing and happiness. The air is polluted beyond a level where we can be healthy, we have unacceptable amounts of child poverty, food banks, widespread and growing homelessness and increasing violence and suicide rates. Hospital emergency units are swamped because people can't get a doctor's appointment, prisoners are rioting in the jails, day care centres for older folk are closing down, libraries are closing down, rubbish collections are fewer and fewer, the roads are full of potholes, the trains don't work, schools are having to get donations from parents to buy books, food banks are overwhelmed and one in four has a mental health issue. There was a time when a single wage would provide enough to maintain a household including kids but now the same household can't get by on even two full time salaries. The upshot of this is that the majority of those on state benefits are people who are in full-time work because they are simply not paid enough to cover the basic essentials. No wonder we are all stressed out. If that is the definition of a strong economy you can keep it mate.

The problem is not limited to the UK. Governments everywhere have completely misunderstood their principle purpose which is of course to keep all their people safe and well. This is closely followed by the sacred task of providing employment and prosperity. Employment for all those who want it and prosperity for all. Somehow though, with only very few exceptions, governments of all types everywhere seem intent principally on two main interests which are: 1. Maintaining their hold on power and 2. Safeguarding the interests of gigantic commercial concerns. In the UK, part of this hopelessly feeble plan involves issuing massive contracts for government services to the private sector so that they, the government, are no longer accountable for anything and have someone else to blame when things go wrong as they inevitably do. Why inevitably? Because when you let private companies run say the national train set they have a different purpose in mind to their customers and a different idea of what is required of them. Their main aim is to make a big profit and provide a fat dividend for shareholders but by the time they take away those very significant sums from the business there is never enough left to run it properly or to invest in the infrastructure and this leads to a situation where staff are underpaid, maintenance is shoddy, rolling stock is crumbling and service generally slides downhill at a rate of knots much faster than the trains themselves. The customers just want the damn trains to run on time but this is a matter conveniently shunted into the siding of no importance for train companies.

The UK rail franchises are a gold mine for those who run and invest in them but a disaster for those who have to use trains to get to work, go on holiday, visit sick relatives or just have a day out somewhere because they are, more often than not, late, uncomfortable, crowded, dirty and slow while the companies running them share out bigger and bigger profits, bonuses and dividends. This is just one example of the way the system we have is unfair to the majority of folk and a veritable gravy train, indeed, an actual gravy train for those few lucky people who enjoy a fantastic life on the proceeds. No wonder we are all stressed out. Yes I know, I have said this before and will very likely say it again because this state of affairs is the same for all the public utilities and it's making us all sick. I mean in all honesty how can you morally apply the profit motive to water? But this is not just a political diatribe, it is an explanation of why the methods in this book are so important in today's world and why I am so motivated to get them out there to those who need them and it is very likely that that includes pretty much just about everybody. I believe it is also reasonable to suggest that it is the political situation that contributes in quite large measure to making the majority of folk stressed, anxious and unhappy when it is supposed to do the exact opposite. If someone is stressed out just getting to work and back every day because the train is late or because their kids' education is lousy or they can't earn enough to pay basic bills or have a decent place to live or eat decent, healthy food etc. then the chances are they will be stressed and unhappy enough to get ill and many, many do. It is a fact that one in four have mental health issues. A truly horrifying statistic. Just have a look around next time you're on a commuter train and see how many happy people you can spot. Most of them look like death warmed up. Is this how it is supposed to be? What life should be like? Is this how people should be treated? Is this how we should treat each other? Not as far as I am concerned. Life should be such a wondrous adventure and we reduce it to a meaningless, ball-aching chore.

Of course, if you're a fund manager or foreign exchange dealer with connections in the cabinet you're probably playing the tables in Monte Carlo and wondering what all the fuss is about. So that's okay then, some of us are doing alright. Despite everything that happens some of us will always be alright. But strangely it is those very kind of people who tend to be regular visitors to my consulting room because their collective anxiety stimulates a recurring nightmare in which the runaway gravy train crashes into the buffers and its precious cargo of rich, pungent sauce leaks away into the ground until it's all soaked into the dirt they lose everything. No matter how much money they have, they want more and this is what they worry about most of all.

Over the years I've had many clients who either run their own businesses or have highly paid positions in industry or banking. I mention that they're highly paid because in most cases that's the only reason they do it. The money. Not because they love it or consider it their life's work. Indeed, in most cases they hate and resent it. But the remuneration keeps them living in a particular style, when they have the time to enjoy it (not a lot), and they much prefer to accept the negative consequences of the deal than switch to a vocation they do like or even feel passionate about for less money.

This folks, is a road to nowhere. They resent the mindless boredom of their working lives that involves dragging themselves out of bed still dog-tired ridiculously early in the morning and leaving home in darkness before the kids are even up. They hate the daily misery of that weary commute, often a couple of hours or more in a crowded, stuffy train, pressed up so close to other sweaty folks that they're almost fornicating. Quite often having to stand for the whole wearisome journey with only a drab, joyless destination devoid of happiness or love at the end of it. They resent the place they work where the moment they walk through the door they are under incessant pressure to get results. Monitored, watched, controlled, tested and judged for the ten, twelve or maybe even sixteen hours they are expected to pour all their energy into a meaningless task that contributes nothing for the benefit of society. Quite the opposite in fact. And then finally, the door opens to admit a crack of light towards which they gravitate like moths. Out towards the light of freedom. Out once again to jostle with the crowds on the crowded journey back home where the kids are already fast asleep and dinner lies dried out in the oven and their partner lies dried out in bed. No wonder they go mad.

Now if you're looking to transform your life and get the better of negative emotions there's absolutely no point in continuing to do the same things as you've done before because obviously nothing will change. If you carry on doing what you're doing then everything will remain the same. Clearly, if you are stressed, angry, anxious, frightened, worried etc. and want to be confident, happy, successful, full of energy etc. and then you have to change something because to achieve what you haven't achieved you need to do what you've never done. When I say achieve, it could mean many things. Business, sport, finances, love, travel, write a book, climb Kilimanjaro, play football for Real Madrid, make a million, go round the world etc. Whatever you want to do, whatever your walk of life, whatever is your aim, purpose, desire, focus, dream, if you're struggling, if you're not happy, if you're stuck in any way at all, there's a reason for it and if you fail to deal with that reason and keep on doing the same things you're doing now you will continue to struggle, be stuck and unhappy. You don't have to take it from me. It's what Einstein said and by all accounts he was quite the clever trousers.

Exercise 10 - Anxiety Zap Tap

Tune in to the issue you're dealing with, stress, anxiety, fear, doubt, worry etc. and assess it on a scale of one to ten. One - not much, ten - a lot.

Take a nice, big deep breath, hold for three seconds and breath out.

Take hold of your wrist with the opposite hand so that your fingers are wrapped around the inside. Take a nice, big deep breath and as you breathe out and say to yourself slowly 'Peace'. Feel a wave of calmness and relaxation.

Now tap in between the eyebrows while saying 'Release and let go'.

Tap the side of the eye while saying 'Release and let go'.

Tap under the eye while saying 'Release and let go'.

Tap on the collarbone point while saying 'Release and let this go'.

Take hold of your wrist with the opposite hand so that your fingers are wrapped around the inside. Take a nice, big deep breath and as you breathe out and say to yourself slowly 'Peace'. Feel that wave of calmness flooding through your body.

Measure the intensity of the issue again on a scale of one to ten and notice how much it has reduced.

Repeat as much as you like if necessary.

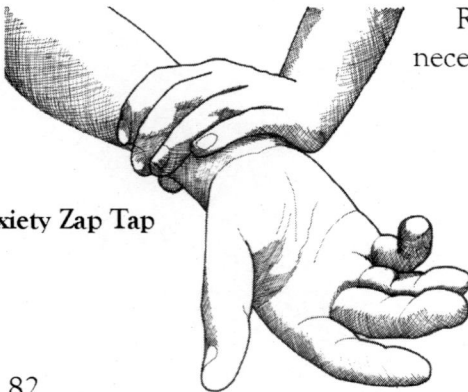

Anxiety Zap Tap

The Potent Cocktail

'Until the philosophy which holds one race superior and another inferior is finally and permanently discredited and abandoned, everywhere is war. And until there are no longer first-class and second-class citizens of any nation, until the colour of a man's skin is of no more significance than the colour of his eyes. And until the basic human rights are equally guaranteed to all without regard to race, there is war. And until that day, the dream of lasting peace, world citizenship, rule of international morality, will remain but a fleeting illusion to be pursued, but never attained... now everywhere is war.' - Haile Selassie (Popularised by Bob Marley in the song 'War')

We tend to worship certain types of glamorous people and some of my clientele are exactly those types. Highly talented in their respective fields, very well paid, good looking, sparkling, vivacious, fit as a butcher's dog and in many cases very, very, very, very unhappy. Yes indeed. You'd be surprised. Please don't assume that wealth, fame and stunning good looks equal happiness and joy because I can assure you they don't albeit it would be wrong to suggest those positive assets don't help at all sometimes. But the simple truth is that those celebrity icon types who we adore so much are in some ways, wait for it, yes, exactly like us. They may appear to be superheroes but when the chips are down it turns out they have the same fears and insecurities as everyone else and much more so in many cases.

Sorry to shatter your illusions but that's the way it is I'm afraid. And yet it doesn't have to be because when unhappy people, whoever they are, learn certain very simple exercises and, frankly, if you can't learn these simple things you're probably doomed anyway, and if they carry them out regularly, five or ten minutes per day is all I'm asking for, then they can feel great and at the height of their powers. Please don't say you haven't got time because you'd be kidding yourself as much as anyone else. Are you seriously saying you can't spare five or ten minutes a day to feel well? So here it is my friends. Here in these pages is the secret key to happiness and success that you've been seeking all your life. What have you got to lose? As I have said, some of the techniques I use with all my clients including premiership footballers, international cricketers and tennis players, CEOs, pop stars and ballet dancers amongst other celebrity types are right here. So you have absolutely no excuses at all and if you follow my advice you'll take advantage of them because it's rare that a collection of such a rich and potent methods drawn from such a range of modalities from such different cultures all around the world is made available in this way. You can easily find books on hypnosis, NLP, tapping etc. because practitioners tend to specialise in one modality or another and want to publish their expertise relating to a particular speciality. Of course, some of these books contain incredibly valuable information albeit within limited parameters but in my opinion the best results are obtained using a cocktail of different methods and for that reason I've gathered a wide range together for you here. Basically, I've done the research for you so that you can enjoy and benefit from my efforts and experience over the last twenty years or so because you have the added knowledge that each of the exercises here has been thoroughly tested and works fantastically well. I never include any method in my repertoire before using it extensively on myself or one of my close associates to be sure of its efficacy. (For instance CBT and Mindful meditation, which are flavour of the month in some circles don't even make the cut as far as my method is concerned).

Also, you can be sure that I have used all the techniques mentioned here very successfully with a cross-section of clients from the very high-achieving to the very down-and-out mostly with quite magical outcomes. Wherever I take these methods they are received with fascination and warm approval and that is the main reason I want to get them out to you and the world. It is a mission. When you have something so good that can change the world for the better then the instinct is to shout from the rooftops about it. Well it's my instinct anyway. So the mantra is very clear, use these exercises every day or at least just the ones you like best and watch your life improve instantly and exponentially. There, I've said it again.

Actually, I would claim that my experience with all these methods is quite unique because amongst a myriad of activities in the field I have worked at fourteen professional UK football clubs and the moment you find yourself in such a position it opens up a new and huge clientele. You have anything up to forty-five players, around half-a-dozen coaches, the Manager, the physios, kit-men, doctor, chaplain, ground staff, possibly fifty academy students, the Board of Directors which can number ten or twelve and the people who work in the office which can be anything from two to fifty depending on the size of the club. When they know you're there and they see what you can do they all start knocking on your door or approaching you surreptitiously in the car park. If you're at the club for any length of time the fans also become aware of your involvement and even some of those guys approach you for sessions. So you walk in to a fairly massive ready-made clientele and this provides the opportunity to test out all sorts of things. Try new modalities, new techniques, invent new methods etc. etc. Of course the players and others in the club have no idea what you're doing and if it works, and it always does, then they're all as happy as Larry. It is a situation I have experienced on numerous occasions and this fairly rigorous trial and error process has enabled me to discover exactly what works best and what doesn't work quite as well. Of course new modalities and methods are surfacing all the time, indeed, I have invented quite a few myself and they all need testing but I never include any techniques in my method until I am absolutely sure of their efficacy and effectiveness. I could be wrong but I doubt very much if any other mental coach has had the same experience because I am not aware of know anyone who has worked at so many clubs or worked with so intensively with so many elite players using so many different modalities.

Having already referred to some of my high-achieving clients I was going to joke that I also have many ordinary clients too. But this really is just a joke and must not be taken seriously because in my world of passionate idealism there are no ordinary people. Every single person is incredibly special and we are all brothers and sisters and all equal. Accordingly, although it sounds contradictory, I have a fee structure ranging from quite a lot to nothing at all because I want everyone, regardless of means, to be able to access these simple methods that can help us all be happier. I'm like a one man NHS. Indeed, at a particular point in my chequered career I decided to award myself a promotion from Mental Performance Coach to Mental Performance Consultant because I felt I had reached a new and higher level in my work that justified it. I work entirely on my own so only I could possibly know that and only I had the authority to sanction my promotion. So now you can access either my NHS type service without having to pay much or request my private, de-luxe service which obviously costs more. Of course, the quality of the work is exactly the same. If you're a premiership footballer, CEO, pop star or a cabinet minister please go straight to the private consultancy.

My advice is don't worship other people like celebrities or footballers because of what they do. Find your own talents and go out and do them yourself. Knock yourself out! Yes you can!

Exercise 11 - Energy Thump

Need a boost of energy?

This is a great way to kick start your chi energy and wake up.

I mean really wake up.

Really I mean now.

Wake up now.

Using both hands tap the ends of your fingers on your chest. To find the points to tap find the v-shaped indent below the neck and come down a few centimetres from there. Please refer to the tapping points diagram. They are the same points we use for the 9-gamut process explained earlier and are called the collarbone points. Tap fairly hard. I tend to call this a thump rather than a tap.

Now tap (or thump) together the sides of the hands called the karate points. If you're in doubt please refer to the tapping point diagram again.

Now thump the collarbone points again.

And now the karate points again.

Feel more energetic? Good.

Feel that tingling?

That's chi energy.

Excellent

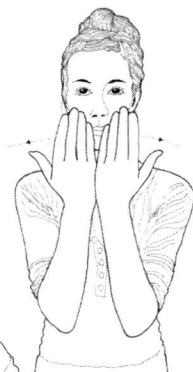
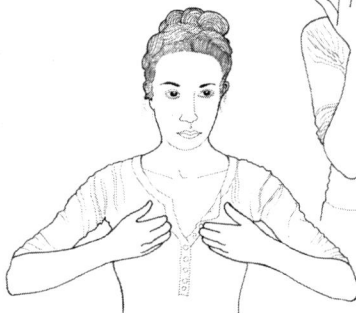
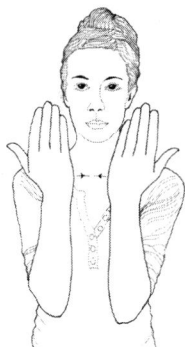

Energy Thump

Quit the Comfort Zone

'If history teaches us anything it is that we continue to make the same mistakes.' - Peter Gilmour

If you want an easy life by which I mean if you're happy with the status quo and don't care to challenge it, don't wish to re-examine your beliefs or have your boat rocked then this book may not be much to help you. But if you want to break new boundaries, explore your mind, go beyond and seek new worlds of understanding and fulfilment then you'll find some great methods in these pages to help you do that. Most people prefer to stay well within their comfort zone where they feel safe and secure. Where they can resist any attempt to challenge the beliefs, institutions, rules and regulations that govern their lives and provide a structure that allows them to feel content albeit with an uneasy tinge. I have never been this way inclined. From an early age I challenged just about everything and even today at a relatively advanced age I am still as idealistic as ever, probably more so. As science and technology progress at breakneck pace we have wonderful inventions that could help us live better, more interesting and fulfilling lives. Albeit after four billion years of development it's depressing to think that some people regard the TV show The X-factor as the height of human achievement. But things seem to be getting worse. Facts show that there are more slaves in the world now than there were during the period in which the film 'Twelve Years a Slave' was set. A shocking statistic unfolding right on our doorstep within touching distance of what we consider civilised society. In the world's largest cities such as London where I sit right now there are actual slaves who have been smuggled in to carry out domestic or industrial chores for long hours with no breaks, no rights, no access to the outside world, little food and no money. Literally gaoled with hard labour by criminals and forced to work all hours on building sites, factories or in the domestic scenario cleaning, cooking and tending to the gaoler's every whim. We use technology in the form of so-called smart weapons to kill more people in greater numbers than ever before. Look at Iraq, Syria, Libya, Sudan, Yemen etc. where war has created a situation in which women and children are slaughtered and raped in great numbers. Does this make us more civilised or less? Happier or less happy? After all, most of the weapons in these areas originate from us and our allies. Weapons we happily sell to dodgy regimes with the full knowledge that they will be passed on to other armies with few scruples. Why should countries like Iran, North Korea, India, Israel and Pakistan spend a fortune on nuclear weapons? Why do they need them anyway? Why should such frighteningly destructive power be needed at all in a modern, civilised world? Can't we find enough reasonable people to reach reasonable agreements to allow all of us to live in peace and harmony? Naive, yes. Simple, yes. Obvious, yes. Logical, yes. What most people want, yes. Can we do it? No. Even my own country the UK which apparently suffers from a weakened economy due to the decision to leave the European Union and other reasons has made a new commitment to its nuclear deterrent for a gigantic cost of tens of billions. How much? Good god, all that money for a thing that can never be used. Is this not the absolute, pure definition of insanity? Have we not seen the pictures of Hiroshima? Have we completely lost the ability to discuss matters reasonably with other nations and reach peaceful agreements to suit us all? That's what most people want and democratic governments are supposed to act on behalf of most people. But the social contract has broken down. We are sick and need to get better. We are all poor men struggling to be free.

Look at pollution in cities like Delhi, Beijing, Mexico City, Rio de Janeiro and even London, Tokyo and Hong Kong. Economies roaring ahead without a single care for the sanctity or sanity of a clean environment or the health of the good folk who live there. What on earth is a government for if not to protect their citizens from toxicity and create a healthy environment? I say unequivocally that this is absolute madness. When will we ever learn? So when I say that I am driven to disseminate these simple methods to people in order to help the world become a happier place with more love between people it may sound naive but it's my small contribution towards reversing the momentum of this nonsense, this utter madness and I invite you to join me and all the other good guys on the side of peace and love. It may mean straying out of your comfort zone but take courage mon brave! There's nothing to fear and the rewards are considerable. Promise.

Where all the good stuff happens

Your comfort zone

The Wheel-spin Theory

Imagine a Tom and Jerry type of cartoon with a character sitting in a red and yellow car pressing hard on the accelerator so that the wheels are spinning fast but mud is flying everywhere, the tyres are wearing down and the car is not moving. This describes to a large extent the way many people feel about their lives. Working hard and putting in huge effort but not going anywhere or at least not getting far. What they need to do is the very opposite of what they're doing. Instead of revving up and wasting huge amounts of energy trying to go as fast as possible, if they just lift their foot partly off the pedal and throttle back a bit then the wheels slow down, the tyres get some grip and the car moves easily and effortlessly forward. Relax is the operative word here.

Here's a method to help you do this.

Exercise 12 - Collarbone Breathing

Place either hand, palm down, on either collarbone point. (See diagram of tapping points on page 131 or to locate your collarbone points find the v-shaped bone below your neck and about three centimetres down and then three centimetres both left and right are your collarbone points.) Raise your thumb to make sure it is not in contact with your body. This is because the thumb has a negative polarity and if it touches your body this amazing exercise will be less successful. Using a couple of fingers of the other hand begin tapping on the gamut spot of the hand on the collarbone point. Keep tapping while you follow these instructions. Breath in. Breath out half. Breathe out fully. Breathe in half. Breathe out. Make a fist with the hand on the collarbone point and place it back on the collarbone point. Thumb out of the way and tap on the gamut spot as before while following the same instructions. Breath in. Breath out half. Breathe out fully. Breathe in half. Breathe out. Now move the hand to the other collarbone point and repeat exactly as before. First with hand flat then with fist. Change hands and repeat the whole exercise on both sides.

Altogether that means going through the breathing sequence a total of eight times. This exercise both relaxes and energises and I heartily recommend it to be done every morning and at any time you face a challenge or need to overcome issues. It is a great exercise to do before bedtime if you want to sleep well.

Mohammed Ali and Self-Talk

'I'm the Greatest!'

Something which is easy to do anywhere, anytime, without anyone noticing and which costs absolutely nothing, however much you do it, is keeping your self-talk nice and strong. Self-talk is the internal dialogue, the way we speak to ourselves and it's very important to make sure to keep it as positive as possible if you want to be happy and achieve great things.

The problem is that we have a tendency to beat ourselves up when we make a mistake or things don't go the way we want them to. We say things to ourselves such as I can't do this or this will never work or I don't feel confident about this. When things go wrong we may call ourselves an idiot (or worse) and talk angrily and critically to ourselves as if trying to prove ourselves guilty of something. It's a bit like the scene in Faulty Towers when Basil Fawlty thrashes his car with the branch of a tree because it won't start. Of course, that's mad behaviour by a fictional character but the principle is the same. Blaming a third party outside ourselves for something which is our own responsibility. Thrashing the car is a substitute for punishing himself.

One thing that helps us stay strong whatever the situation is to say positive things to ourselves. I can do this and I will do this. I feel good. I feel strong, confident and powerful. I'm a winner. I can succeed and I will succeed etc. etc. The reason for this is that whatever you say to yourself travels along neural pathways into your unconscious mind which is uncritical and believes everything you tell it. Therefore, say positive things to yourself. These strongly worded sentences are called affirmations. Imagine what you want to happen not what you fear might happen. If you tell yourself you're an idiot that's what the unconscious mind believes and it just compounds the issue. Tell yourself you're really great and see how your life changes for the better!

Similarly, if you imagine doing great things such as scoring great goals in football or completing a valuable contract in business or performing well on the stage or just being great in a meeting or interview, anything which is a challenge, you will find yourself performing really well. This is because anything you imagine travels along those neural pathways into the unconscious mind which doesn't differentiate between reality and imagination so it registers that you've actually done all the great things you imagine doing. Of course if you've done them once you can do them again and this gives you confidence. This is the principle behind visualisation in sport but unknown to most coaches it works a thousand times better when you carry it out it in a light hypnotic trance. It also works in every other field of endeavour, not just sport.

The simple fact (and all the best things in life are simple) is that the unconscious mind has the power to influence the actions of the body and by using certain simple techniques you will not only lift your sporting, business, artistic performance level but your life will improve generally. Try it. Keep your self-talk nice and strong and see how your life improves. Instead of saying 'I can't do this.' Or 'It'll never work.' Say 'I can do it and I will do it.' In your mind's eye see yourself succeeding, winning, achieving your goal. See yourself doing whatever you need to do in order to be successful and you probably will.

It is vitally important for the athlete, the business person, the artist, singer, entertainer or anyone else who is interested in success of any sort or anyone who just wants to be content and happy to keep their self-talk nice and strong in the way described above. Indeed, this may in some cases be the only difference between success and failure. This is something which is easy to do anywhere, anytime, without anyone noticing and which costs absolutely nothing however much you do it. Self-talk is the internal dialogue, the way we speak to ourselves and it's very important to keep it nice and positive as much as possible if you want to be happy and achieve great things.

One of the best exponents of the art of positive self-talk was the legendary boxer Cassius Clay, later Mohammed Ali who went around proclaiming 'I'm the greatest' before anyone had even heard of him. And what happened to him? He became the heavyweight boxing champion of the world and one of the most impressive, admired and loved athletes the world has ever seen including amongst those who don't even like boxing. That's what positive self-talk can do for you. So remember, say I'm the greatest not I'm an idiot and you can be champion of the world!

Exercise 13 - Be Nice to Yourself

Remember, if you make a mistake you should resist the urge to call yourself an idiot or denigrate yourself in other ways because your sub-conscious mind will hear and believe what you are saying and thinking compounding the issue and causing those negative thoughts and beliefs to become part of your inner realities and affect you in a negative way. You should say to yourself things like: 'I feel strong, confident and powerful.' 'I can do better and I will do better.' 'I'm a winner.' Etc. These positive thoughts and intentions will travel down neural pathways into the sub-conscious mind and replace the negative ideas in there such as 'I'm an idiot'.

Say out loud now: 'I will never say anything bad about myself ever again.' That's it. Done.

Power Pose

*'A healthy body means a healthy mind. You get your heart rate up
and you get the blood flowing through your body to your brain. Look
at Albert Einstein. He rode a bicycle. He was also an early student of
Jazzercise. You never saw Einstein lift his shirt but he had a six-pack
under there'* - Steve Carell

Body Language follows the same principle as self-talk but
concerns the way others perceive us. In sport, the competitor's
body language should remain strong and powerful whatever
happens and particularly when the momentum may be against
them. That's a temporary situation and can change at any
moment. Whatever the situation, whatever the score, whatever
they feel, whatever's being thrown at them they must continue
to display a calm, relaxed, positive and totally confident image to
the opponent. Adopt a power pose. Totally aware and focussed.
Relaxed but ready. No temper, no wasted energy, no tantrums,
no sulking, no shouting, no fear, no anxiety, no stress. Head up,
arms swinging, steely gaze, in control, on top, focussed, smiling,
strong, confident, powerful and happy at all times. No exceptions.
And that goes for whatever you're doing or walk of life you may be
involved in. There was a Hypnotherapist called Milton Erickson.

Actually, he wasn't just any old Hypnotherapist, he was the
granddaddy of all Hypnotherapists. Every Hypnotist working
today owes something to Erickson because he was a pioneer of the
art, a creative innovator, a great man. Erickson told many stories,
it was his style of Hypnosis, and there are many stories about him
too. One is about a time he treated a client for depression and
after the session instructed the client on his way home to count
all the chimneys on the houses and to call him with the total. A
strange request indeed but Erickson was an innovator and there
was always method in his ostensible madness because what he

wanted was for his client to look up. The simple fact is that if you look up and keep your gaze above your eye-line it lifts your mood. Depressed or unhappy people tend to look down. So this is what I say to all my clients. Look up, smile and feel better.

Vivid Visualisation

'Imagine what you want to happen. Not what you fear might happen.' - Peter Gilmour

Visualisation, sometimes referred to as mental rehearsal, is at least one technique known and used by some UK sports coaches and is a simple, highly effective exercise that can also be used in any other field of endeavour. The way it works is that if you imagine as vividly as possible what it feels, looks and sounds like to have a successful outcome to any particular goal, the thoughts you imagine travel along neural pathways into the always open, uncritical, unconscious mind which doesn't differentiate between what's real and what's imagined and therefore registers that you have actually achieved whatever you imagined. This could be anything such as scoring goals in cup finals, winning massive business contracts, being Wimbledon champion, appearing as the principle dancer at the Royal Ballet or of course, getting laid. Although it's worth paying attention where the last one is concerned because when you visualise things deeply in a hypnotic trance, which is really the best and only way to do this properly, the body tends to respond with all the associated muscle movements. You can often feel your muscles moving and twitching unconsciously in response as you carry out this exercise even though it's purely imaginary. The point is that if you've done it once you can do it again and this gives you confidence. Wimbledon 1978 champion Pat Cash said he visualised the whole of his victorious final match on the previous night so he felt like he had already been there and done when when he stepped on to the court to play the match even though he had no actual experience of winning a grand slam tournament final. Imagine yourself playing well, being a champion, winning, signing a big contract, getting that job, dancing, singing, acting or playing a musical instrument perfectly. Making an inspirational speech that turns everyone on. Playing fantastic shots, scoring great goals, jumping higher, running faster, collecting the trophy etc. If there's an area of your performance whatever your walk of life or profession that needs improvement (if not there's absolutely no point in you reading this anyway) imagine performing that function in a technically perfect way, exactly the way you want to and then the information concerning exactly how to perform that function will be recorded in your sub-conscious mind ready to be triggered whenever you need it.

In the famous basketball experiment on visualisation conducted by Dr. Blaslotto at the University of Chicago in 1996 a group of students who had been randomly selected were asked to take a series of free throws and their success rate percentage was noted. They were then divided into three groups and asked to perform three separate tasks over a thirty-day period. The first group was told not to touch a basketball for thirty days, no practicing or playing basketball whatsoever. The second group was told to practice shooting free throws for half an hour a day for thirty days. The third group was to come to the gym every day for thirty days and spend half an hour with their eyes closed, simply visualizing hitting every free-throw. After the thirty days all three groups were asked to come back and take the same number of free-throws they had in the beginning of the study to check on their progress. The results were as follows:

The first group of students who did not practice at all showed no improvement. The second group had practiced every day and showed a 24% improvement. The third group which had simply visualized successful free-throws, showed a 23% improvement. In other words, the improvement in the group that purely visualized the exercise was virtually the same as the group who had physically practiced. The conclusion here is that if you visualise success before starting any activity your chances of being successful are much greater.

In fact, this experiment has been duplicated at various learning establishments around the world with similar results everywhere. Visualize yourself as a successful person in whichever way you desire and spend a few minutes each and every day shaping that person you want to become into your subconscious mind. Without any doubt at all this is the way it is going to be. This will also sharpen your concentration skills, your will power and bring you closer to achieving your aims. Visualisation is an excellent and very useful technique to utilise. Imagine doing great things such as scoring great goals in football or completing valuable contracts in business or performing well on the stage, moving into that dream house you always wanted or just being great in a meeting or interview, anything which is a challenge, and you will find yourself performing really well in actuality because anything you imagine travels along those neural pathways into the unconscious mind which doesn't differentiate between what's real and what's imagined so it registers that you've actually done all those great things you imagined doing. Of course if you've done them once you can do them again and this gives you confidence. This is the principle behind visualisation in sport and of course it works just as well in every other area of life. But generally unknown to many people it works a thousand times better when done in a light hypnotic trance. It also works in any other field of endeavour, not just sport. So imagine yourself signing that valuable contract, working in your dream job at the place you want to work, living in your dream house with your dream partner, having more money and living the dream. Imagine it vividly in self-hypnosis and it creates the vibration that resonates on the same level as that which you desire. A vibration that draws it to you.

Visualisation is an immensely valuable technique when carried out in the waking state but is a thousand times better, stronger, more vivid and effective when guided by a facilitator in hypnosis.

Exercise 14 - Self-Hypnosis

Yes you can do it yourself and this is how:

This is a fairly simple procedure but it needs a longer explanation than some of the other exercises. I urge you to learn and use self-hypnosis in your life because it is worth finding the time to do it which only needs to be five minutes but can be half an hour.

Self-hypnosis is a wonderful tool for a variety of applications. It is perfectly safe, entirely free and produces amazing results. In my opinion that's a pretty good deal. A win, win, win situation with nothing whatsoever to lose and a great deal to gain. If you ignore it after that glowing recommendation you've got bigger problems that you thought mate. Really though, I encourage you with all my passion and strength to take up this method because it will improve your life without question. I encourage all my clients to do it whether they have any issues or not. But not everyone finds the time. It is a shame.

In particular, you can use it to reduce stress, anxiety, fear, doubt, worry etc. Or to boost confidence, belief, focus, motivation, energy, success and happiness. If you have problem sleeping it will help you sleep. If you're in pain it will take it away or at least help to reduce it. If you need to relax, and who doesn't? It will help you chill right out to levels you have never before experienced. Indeed, it has so many wonderful properties that it's hard to believe it's entirely legal.

Some people are paying out a small fortune for substances that can't do even a fraction of what hypnosis can. In the world of sport for instance, some unscrupulous athletes ingest mountains of powders and potions in an effort to raise performance levels when they could be using hypnosis which is not only legal but completely safe also not to mention great, great fun. Just think of the damage using drugs can do. If you're found out it could be the end of your career and god knows what you're doing to your body with that stuff. Why on earth take such a massive risk when you can use something a thousand times better and safer from every point of view?

Self-hypnosis (or any kind of hypnosis for that matter) is very effective in the alleviation of stress and tension, in helping to regulate sleeping patterns and for focusing on goals. Self-hypnosis is the ability to focus your energy on creating a self-induced, relaxed state of mind and body. When you are in a trance state you can focus your energy on a specific goal or simply quieten the mind and enter a state of deep mental and physical relaxation.

So first find a quiet place where you won't be disturbed and sit or lie down comfortably. Dim the lights or turn them off. Some like to light a candle or burn some aromatherapy oils and it is okay to employ anything that helps you to create a relaxing atmosphere but it's not strictly necessary. You can do it anywhere at any time and you don't really need anything else. My favourite place is on a lounger after a sauna at my gym. Turn off your phone. I said TURN THE BLOODY THING OFF. You heard. Once you get skilled at self-hypnosis you can use it in busy places where there are noises and distractions. With practise you will find it easy to block out distractions and still be able to focus your mind intently. As with all the various techniques in this book, the more you practice the better you get at doing them. Indeed, that's the same with any other skill in life.

Tell yourself that you are going to practise self-hypnosis and work out how long you want to spend on it. Fifteen or twenty minutes is probably about right to start with but as you become more proficient, it could be longer or shorter. What on earth does that mean? Well as you train yourself to enter a hypnotic trance quicker you eventually find you can do it in seconds so you spend less time on the exercise. However, after a little practise you may also decide to make your session last longer because you become more familiar with being in a trance and enjoy it more as you find out how to make better use of it for longer. Confused? Yes, so am I.

Decide what issue you want to work on. In my experience it's better to work on one at a time rather than lining up everything in your life you want to solve such as stopping smoking, losing weight, getting rid of fears or phobias, building confidence etc. I mean you can't do it all at once. I mean you allow all these negative traits to build up all your life and can't be bothered to do anything about it and now you think you can get rid of it all in five minutes. I mean please, be reasonable. What do you think this is? Black magik? Pick one. Goddamit. Pick one to start with and be grateful you can even get that. Be patient, Did you hear me? I said BE PATIENT FOR CHRIST'S SAKE. Only kidding x. Construct some affirmations that relate to the issue such as I am a non-smoker, I feel confidence flooding through my body and mind, I feel calm, relaxed and comfortable in a lift, I can do this and I will do this etc. etc. Invent some strongly worded affirmations that relate to the subject you're dealing with and mean something to you and have them ready for when they are required. Not now. I'll tell you when. Close your eyes and take a couple of nice, big deep breaths down into the diaphragm. Remember, breathing in relaxation and calmness, breathing out stress, anxiety and any nervous tension. Clear your mind but don't worry if you still get any unwanted thoughts in your mind because they will soon drift away again just as easily as they came. Go round the body relaxing each muscle group in turn. Start at the top of the head and let all the muscles around your scalp go loose, limp and lazy. Then the muscles round the eyes, nose, mouth etc. Make a point of relaxing the jaw muscles because they are some of the strongest and most tense muscles in the body. We use them for talking, chewing, biting and smiling etc. so focus on them for a moment and make sure they are nice and relaxed. Go round the arms, hands, torso, pelvic area, upper legs, lower legs etc. etc. right to the very tips of your toes. Relax all those muscles and by the time you have done that you will be in a pretty relaxed state all over.

Next, start counting down slowly from twenty down to zero becoming twice as relaxed with each number you count. Feel every muscle in your body relax more and more with each descending number. To enhance this relaxing effect at the same time as counting you can imagine you are travelling down in an elevator or walking down steps into a beautiful garden or flying down to land in an aeroplane or riding down an escalator or skiing or sledging down a beautiful mountain maybe. The thing is to imagine going down, that's the thing. By the time you get to zero you'll be in a light hypnotic trance and ready to introduce those affirmations. Use whatever feels right for you. Being in a trance is a very subtle feeling and you don't always realise you're in one until you're there. The more you practise the better you will get at it and in time, you will begin to know intuitively when you are in a deeper, more receptive state. As you practice, you'll build up your expertise and find yourself slipping into trance quicker and easier. Feel relaxed about going into a deep state of trance. It is a wonderful experience which will take you to a powerful part of yourself where you can make big changes. Allow yourself to go deep inside your mind and tell yourself you feel safe and secure as you do this. Can you get stuck in a trance? People often ask this and the answer is no. But anyway it's nothing to worry about because it would be wonderful if you could. Everything would flow easily and effortlessly and you'd have a great time achieving all your aims. It is important to stress that no harm can come to you with hypnosis. Only good things happen. Sometimes you may drift into a restful sleep while doing this but in this case you can just wake up in your own time as you would from a regular sleep. When you are nice and relaxed and floaty is the time to bring in those affirmations. The main point about affirmations is to make sure they are strong and positive and in the present. Say them to yourself a few times and really feel them as you repeat them to yourself. Draw them inside you and let every cell in your mind and body resonate with positive feelings and emotion. Imagine every part of you is repeating the affirmations with complete conviction and total belief in what you are stating. Remember: your unconscious mind believes exactly what it is told. You are creating new positive beliefs that will be accepted by your unconscious exactly as they are, without any analysis because it is completely uncritical. You will be surprised at how effective a suggestion can be even in the lightest of trances. The power of the unconscious mind works in a very subtle way. You can also use visualisation when in the trance state. For example, if you are due to go for an interview and you have been feeling nervous, you can visualise yourself going for the interview feeling composed and full of confidence and conducting yourself in a very positive way. Feeling totally in control of the situation. Get a picture of this in your mind. Make the whole picture bright and clear and use as many of your senses as you can, the more vivid your imagination the better. Most importantly, always see yourself in a completely positive light, expressing yourself clearly and confidently and feeling very calm and composed under any pressure. See yourself getting that job. Shaking hands with your interviewers as they say 'Well done, congratulations. You were the best candidate by far.' You can use this powerful technique to prepare yourself for many things, such as an exam of any kind, a sporting event, public speaking, on business and social occasions, even on a romantic date. Remember - your unconscious mind cannot differentiate between what is real and what is imagined, so the more you imagine a positive future situation or event the more you compound your inner belief that you are calm, confident and in control in these situations. Please see the section on visualisation which explains more about what is happening to the mind as you do this.

The more you repeat the affirmations the more the unconscious mind believes them and the more they become true. When you feel it is time to wake up from the trance, all you need to do is to slowly count up from one to ten becoming a bit more awake with each number. When you reach the number ten, your eyes will open and you will be wide-awake with a feeling of total well-being. However much time you had decided to spend on this - ten, fifteen, twenty, thirty minutes I guarantee when you open your eyes it will be right on the dot of that time because the unconscious mind always knows what time it is and will act on your instruction to wake at that point. Enjoy the process and practice as much as you can because like every other skill in life the more you practice the better you become. If you do self-hypnosis before going to sleep there is no need to count up from one to ten because you can simply drift straight off to sleep. Just tell yourself before your session that the trance will turn into a deep, natural sleep from which you will wake in the morning feeling positive and refreshed.

Worry Curry

Pack up your troubles in your old kit-bag
and smile, smile, smile
While you've a lucifer to light your fag
Smile, boys, that's the style
What's the use of worrying? It never was worthwhile
So pack up your troubles in your old kit-bag
and smile, smile, smile

How much do you worry? How many hours per day do you spend worrying about problematic things in your life? An hour, two, three, four hours, more? The average answer is about three hours a day although this is not a totally scientific number. Most say two hours while some say three, four or more. Of course no one knows exactly but that doesn't really matter. Let's say you worry on average about two hours a day. That's fourteen hours a week. About 60 hours per month. 728 hours a year and, wait for it, yes an amazing 7,280 every ten years. Now we all know worrying doesn't help in any way at all. I know we all know that because the people who tell me they worry a lot also tell me they know it doesn't help. This begs the question why on earth do they do it and of course the answer is they can't help it. They'd feel guilty if they didn't worry about the issue they were worrying about even though it is a completely useless waste of energy. So they've never tried to stop it and they have never met me before. I am drawn to the conclusion that deep down people probably enjoy worrying but they insist they don't so let's avoid getting embroiled in the murky matters of the mind otherwise known as dark psychological tendencies and see what we can do to help.

So we have established that you spend a gargantuan seven thousand hours doing something you freely admit is a waste of time when you could be having fun. Watching football, reading, knitting, climbing Kilimanjaro, baking a cake (or maybe seven thousand cakes), or even dare I say, having sex. Although even I would probably agree that seven thousand hours of sex is a bit excessive. (Perhaps optimistic is a better word in my case).

So here is my offer. Hand over all your worrying to me and I'll do it for you so that you can be free to enjoy yourself doing anything you want including having any kind of sex. And if seven thousand hours is a lot (it is) then let me just add that doing it with seven thousand different partners is an even greater challenge and raises even more complicated issues. However, it would almost certainly lead to an entry in the Guinness Book of Records always assuming of course that you could prove it. All things considered however, I feel there's no reasonable doubt that it would take your mind off whatever you were worrying about.

So that's it then. No need to worry anymore because I'm going to do it for you.

How will I do it? Well I'm very good at it you see so I can get through it all in a fraction of the time it takes you. I've spent many years building a worrying expertise, practising, reading books about it, attending courses and I'm now qualified right up to level four which is the highest worry level. This allows me to train others so I have a huge staff of great people who I have trained up to a very high standard and now are very good at worrying too. Obviously not as good as me but really not bad at all. Between us we will do all your worrying for you so you can go out and have a good time. Or stay in and have a good time if you know what I mean. Nudge, nudge, wink, wink say no more! Don't worry about it. By the way, if you find you're still worrying while we are doing your worrying for you, don't worry. We'll just add it to your account for next time. Also, by the way, we also offer a stress, anxiety and trauma service too if it's something that would help. It's a higher level of expertise so it costs a bit more but don't have nightmares we're open to negotiation. (Actually, coping with nightmares is another service we offer). And if you feel guilty about not worrying, don't worry. We have a guilt suffering service too. Yes, we will feel guilty for you while we do your worrying and everyone will wonder why you're always smiling!

The Policeman and the Blind Man

Energy flows where attention goes

When I was a lad, my Dad, god rest him, used to tell a story that still resonates with me today. Whenever I tell it to the various different kinds of audiences who attend my events it resonates with them too. It's about a policeman walking on his beat at night (that gives you a clue as to how far it dates back) when he sees a man on all fours underneath a street lamp apparently searching for something. So the officer approaches the man and asks him what he's doing.

'Looking for my contact lense.' He says.

'Where did you lose it?' Asks the policeman.

'Over there somewhere.' Says the man, gesticulating in a far off direction.

'So why are you looking here then?' Asks the policeman.

'Because there's a light here.' Says the man pointing up at the street lamp.

Now there's a clear moral to this story which is of course that we look in the wrong places for answers to the important issues in life because we are attracted by shining lights that divert our attention. The most powerful of these lights emanates from our TV set. Karl Marx said that religion was the opium of the masses but if he were alive today I'm pretty sure he would be saying that television has superseded religion by a great distance although television itself is now being superseded by the mobile phone.

I have a client who I'm treating for a particular disorder where he tends to drift off into a trance of his own making as opposed to one I might induce. One minute he's there with you, the next his eyes glaze over and he's gone. You might be having an interesting conversation with him and suddenly he just seems to drift away somewhere and shuts down all communication with the outside world. When this happens it's incredibly difficult to break through and get him back again. It's more like a spell than a trance and no amount of finger snapping and loud clapping seems to break it. Every now and then a word will resonate, his eyes will open and he drifts back into consciousness with a quizzical expression as if to ask 'Where have I been?' This happened recently with me clapping and snapping my fingers and shouting his name all to no avail. Even a prod or two had no effect. But then his mobile phone which he had placed on the table in front of us made a ding sound to signal he had a message and he immediately snapped into full conscious awareness, picked up the phone and automatically started to type a reply totally oblivious to the fact I had been furiously trying to rouse him for ten minutes.

Clearly, it seems we have become programmed to respond more to these little magic machines than anything else even the human voice. But the point is that the knowledge we seek is not available on the TV or the internet or in our mobile phones even though we are encouraged to believe it is. Hours and hours of searching the net and watching the box is simply a diversion from the truth and only fills our minds with crass nonsense that is useless to us even though we pretend it's so incredibly important while we're doing it. In the rush hour on the tubes and buses you see rows of people staring intently into their little devices and I used to think they were working. Checking and answering emails, reading professional material, communicating with colleagues etc. all with a really serious expression. I think that's what fooled me because a closer look reveals that they are mostly playing games. A few years ago they took a snapshot of activity on the thousands of computers at one of our largest companies in London city and discovered that over seventy percent of employees were playing solitaire. Our minds are hopelessly addicted to the puerile nonsense constantly streaming into our systems and which, in our search for knowledge, we mistakenly consider important when it is merely a total waste of time. People seem to think they are building up expertise in a valuable, worldly skill of some sort when all they are actually doing is building up a skill at the particular game they are playing. Like killing loads of electronic soldiers with an electronic ray gun for instance. This is all part of the toxic effect discussed in a previous chapter. Not just the banal content which stunts our brains but the blue light emitted by the screens that mesmerise our whole existence. I suggest a different kind of mesmerism is called for.

The knowledge we seek is available in abundance. However, in certain books and certain films and in art and in music and in peoples' eyes and even more so deep down inside ourselves but these are usually the last places we look. If you're reading this book now (and I know you are) then you are one of a tiny minority of good folk who seek the real truth. Welcome to the club.

Exercise 15 - The Leaning Lenny Test

Any Doubt - Leave it Out

This is a way to find out which substances are good for you and which are not. It is a very simple test but one you can trust because it relies on the sub-conscious mind to provide the answers you're seeking. The more we trust in the power of our subconscious mind the better life becomes. I've said this before and please don't be surprised if I say it again because it is crucial for happiness and fulfilment. Not seeking help from some outside, magical deity but finding the answers you need inside. Everything you could possibly want to know is inside you.

To start, take a nice, big deep breath, hold it a few seconds and breathe out again. Tap your third eye point about ten times. Now stand up straight with your feet about eighteen inches apart. Imagine drinking a glass of pure, fresh water. As you imagine drinking the water check which way your body leans. Forward or backwards. Now stand in the same position and imagine drinking a glass of bleach. See which way your body leans this time. Forwards or backwards. Normally if we imagine drinking or eating something that is good for us we tend to lean slightly forwards. If it's something bad for us we lean backwards. So when you imagined drinking water you will probably have leaned forwards and with the bleach, backwards.

We can now start experimenting with all kinds of other things to check whether they are good for us or not and whether they contain toxins. If they're okay you lean forward and if they're harmful in any way you lean backwards. Some people have allergies to such things as nuts, tomatoes, milk (lactose), wheat (gluten) etc. If that is you and you imagine eating or drinking those things or anything containing them you will most likely lean backwards because the body instinctively knows what's good or bad for you.

If something is full of toxins it will have the same effect even if it is something you had previously thought was okay. Therefore, to check if things are good or bad for you imagine eating or drinking them and see which way you lean. Should you have more coffee, beer, pizza, chips, meat, fruit, bread today? Do the leaning Lenny test and your body will tell you.

As you go round the supermarket check what is good or bad for you by doing this simple test. Does it contain something that will have an adverse effect on you? Do the test and find out. Trust your unconscious mind to let you know so that you don't eat something that makes you feel ill without knowing and you do eat things that make you feel great.

Sometimes the test goes the opposite way so that good things make you lean backwards and vice versa. There could be two reasons for this. 1. You have something called polarity reversal (PR) a condition explained earlier which plays havoc with your energy systems. To correct this do the happy tapping exercise from page 22 or alternatively just tap on both karate points and on your upper lip and under your bottom lip. This is known as the PR triangle and tapping on these points will give you an instant lift. Then check the leaning Lenny test again and you will probably find a positive difference because your chi energy is now flowing correctly. 2. The other slight possibility is that you're different. A few people just seem to have a slightly different physiology and react in a slightly different way to these tests but it is unlikely. In many years of doing this with hundreds of people there have only been very few indeed where this has happened. Maybe half a dozen. Like all the exercises here, the leaning Lenny test works with most of the people most of the time and you can rely on it. Of course, if you have a serious allergy to something it might be life-threatening to ingest you must take every precaution to avoid it. The motto here is 'Any doubt - leave it out!'

Walking the Plank

'In this day and age advertising is the way to sell the product and our product is peace.' - John Lennon

If I placed a wooden plank on a carpeted floor and asked you to walk along it you you'd probably have no problem balancing from one end to the other. However, if I placed the same plank across the windows of two adjacent buildings high up on the twentieth floor and asked you to walk across it the task would become entirely different and much more difficult. In fact, it's exactly the same task but because you imagine falling a great distance on to the hard surface of the street below it causes fear to set in. Maybe you'll slip, maybe the plank will break, maybe the wind will blow you off. And before long you imagine yourself lying in a pool of blood on the ground far below. With the security of the soft carpet immediately beneath you have no fear about falling so you skip across the plank easily. But high up there on the twentieth floor there is no such security and your mind focuses only on the drop to oblivion. Logically you should be able to skip across the plank as if it were on the carpet because the task is exactly the same but now you can't even step on to the plank to attempt this very simple prospect of walking along it. The only difference in these two examples is of course the mental approach.

It's called the fight or flight syndrome and it's exactly the same syndrome faced by a professional athlete, a business executive, a singer, dancer or entertainer or anyone else when faced with a challenge such as stepping on to the pitch or the stage or into the boardroom to perform.

It's as if a tiger had jumped into the room and you freeze for a moment while you decide what to do, whether to fight it or run away. It's a common syndrome. For example, professional athletes perform beautifully well in practice but can't always maintain the same level in competition. A business executive may practice his delivery perfectly in front of the mirror and then feel as if someone has torn the tongue from his mouth when he enters the boardroom. It's the fear of failure or fear of making a mistake. Fear that you will look or sound like a fool. In training mistakes don't matter, winning doesn't matter but in competition they do.

So we need techniques to get us through these times. Techniques to ensure we handle those vital moments of competition perfectly. Techniques that will allow us to be champions of walking the plank.

The very first thing is to imagine what you want to happen. Not what you fear might happen. Then follow all the various instructions right here in these pages and everything will be okay. Promise

The Joy of Hypnosis

'An entire sea of water can't sink a ship unless it gets inside the ship. Similarly, the negativity of the world can't put you down unless you allow it to get inside you.' - Goi Nasu

Hypnosis is a state of deep relaxation during which it is possible to communicate with the unconscious mind and replace negative ideas with positive suggestions. The unconscious or sub-conscious mind is where behaviour patterns are created. The process is perfectly safe, very enjoyable and highly effective. The hypnotic state is a pleasant experience which is familiar to us all and similar to daydreaming. It doesn't control your mind or change your character but is highly motivating and very often life-changing in a positive way.

Hypnotherapy, which is hypnosis for therapy, has many applications and is a suitable treatment for such issues as stopping smoking, losing weight, boosting confidence, building self-esteem, boosting energy, relaxation, removing fears, phobias & habits, stress relief, pain relief, anxiety relief, calming exam and driving test nerves, business motivation, managing anger and depression, removing addictions, controlling IBS symptoms, defeating dyslexia, improving concentration etc. etc. Apart from the use of hypnosis for sports motivational purposes, many of these applications are useful to athletes with personal issues to resolve as I know only too well from my own experience.

Hypnosis is sometimes described as an altered state or a state of intense focus. It is a state with which we are all familiar as we experience such states many times during the course of a day particularly when waking in the morning or drifting off to sleep at night because it is the state in between being asleep and awake. A universally familiar hypnotic state is when driving and not being aware of the passage of time. Arriving somewhere without being able to remember how you got there. Some find it frightening but it's perfectly safe because the sub-conscious mind contains the blueprint of how to drive your car from many repeated applications so when the conscious mind drifts into an altered state wandering wherever it will, the subconscious mind automatically takes over and drives the car for you. Should anything happen that requires the driver's attention such as traffic lights changing or the brake lights of the car in front lighting up then the driver simply snaps into conscious awareness and is able to deal with the situation normally.

Hypnotherapy is not the same as stage hypnosis and subjects are never required to do anything embarrassing, reveal any private information or do anything they don't want to do. During hypnotherapy the subject is always in control and aware of everything that happens. You can't get stuck in a trance and can leave it at will. Even if the therapist left the room and never returned you'd simply come round by yourself in a few moments or drift off into a restful sleep.

It is the same with self-hypnosis, the self-induced state that I teach all my clients and encourage them to use regularly. Should anything happen that requires your immediate attention during a session you simply snap into conscious awareness and can deal with it normally.

During Hetro-Hypnosis (that means with a hypnotist facilitating the session) the subject is seated, fully-clothed in a comfortable chair or lying on a couch or prone on the floor (sometimes more convenient with group sessions) listening to the sound of the therapist's voice with a background of soothing music. It is sometimes necessary to respond with finger movements, nods of the head or speech. There is usually no need for physical contact however with the subject's permission the therapist may on certain occasions shake hands, press lightly on the subject's forehead, touch the subject's shoulder or hand or pull or lift their arm.

People turning up for their first Hypnotherapy session are sometimes apprehensive because they have no idea what's going to happen, what it will or should feel like and most likely might have seen some daft stage hypnosis in which participants, often merry with alcohol, are invited on to the stage to be hypnotised and then carry out various quite comic actions under the direction of the hypnotist who appears to control them. Accordingly, people can be concerned about losing control, making a fool of themselves, acting like a chicken, or getting stuck in a trance. Such anxieties are completely baseless. Stage hypnosis is purely for entertainment whereas hypnotherapy is exactly what the word implies, using hypnosis for therapy and is carried out by competent, qualified practitioners who are bound by the ethics and regulations of the profession. Nobody will make a fool of themselves, reveal any private information or lose control. Accordingly therefore, people are never apprehensive for their second session because they have already discovered that it's a relaxing, enjoyable, highly motivational and very beneficial experience and can't wait to get on with it. Clients arriving for a second session often tell me that everywhere they went after the first session people asked them 'Why are you smiling?'

Are there any side effects you ask? Yes, there are. You feel great, totally confident, at the height of your powers and if you play sport your performance level improves. Those are the side effects.

Indeed, nothing bad can happen to you. Only good things happen with hypnotherapy.

Crazy Paradox

'Being in top mental shape requires regular mental training just as being in top physical shape requires regular physical training.' - Peter Gilmour

If you ask any serious athlete to what extent their mental state affects performances they all tell you a huge amount usually seventy, eighty or ninety percent. In the old days at my mental skills workshops I used to go round the room asking each participant for their estimation of this and after hundreds of such occasions I can report that nobody ever gave me a figure of less than fifty percent. But if you then ask those same folks what they do to prepare their minds for competition most of them say nothing at all. This is a crazy paradox because if athletes believe their mental state is such a crucial aspect of performances, at least fifty percent, then logic suggests they should be spending as much time working on their minds as their bodies. But although these legions of ambitious athletes torture themselves with long hours of physical hard slog in the gym, pool, court or field in order to crank up their bodies to peak performance level they do little if anything to condition their minds for competition. The mental side of things is almost completely neglected and many athletes only seek help for mental issues when something goes seriously wrong such as a dramatic loss of form or a crisis of confidence (or both). But without any doubt you need to be mentally strong to make it as a successful athlete. In my work with footballers I have discovered that many English Premiership clubs do not employ any mental training in their coaching programmes and I find this astounding. For those who have that burning ambition please do remember that the world is littered with the broken dreams of talented individuals who lacked the mental strength to achieve the success expected of them. The truth of course is that mental training should form an integral part of the training programme of any athlete who is genuinely interested in success because all the time and effort practicing and getting physically fit is wasted without the mental strength to be composed, confident and properly focussed at vital moments of competition. Deep down they know this. You don't go to the gym once and declare yourself fit. You build up fitness over a period and maintain it regularly with continuous exercise. The same applies to mental strength but it is amazing how many athletes think that a single session of mental training will get their minds 'sorted out'. Whilst you certainly experience a very significant benefit from the first session using my methods it is important to note that it is only a beginning, a tiny glimpse of fabulous future possibilities and that using mind-strengthening methods as a regular part of your training schedule will transport you into new realms of achievement beyond your wildest dreams. In fact, it should be continually stated until indelibly emblazoned on the mind of all athletes and coaches that a programme of mental training should be undertaken by all athletes of any level every day to get their minds in top mental shape in the same way as they undertake physical training every day to get their bodies in top physical shape. There, I've said it again.

Also, just as athletes perform a physical warm-up routine prior to competition, they need a mental warm-up to drive out all negative thoughts and leave them feeling strong, confident and powerful with only positive thoughts flowing through their minds. Few, however, are aware of even the most fundamental techniques for conditioning their minds in this way and labour under the illusion that wearing their lucky underpants, having the same breakfast on match days or listening to their favourite pop music will transport them to world-class heights. Sometimes they ask me for my opinion on these things which basically amount to nothing more than superstition and my answer is always the same. If you think it helps then do it. Whatever you think helps, do it. But make sure you do my stuff as well because these superstitious conventions such that you see many professional athletes indulging in are mere kids-stuff compared to proper mental training methods such as those I suggest in these pages. Unfortunately, athletes are not always assisted much by coaches, many of whom fail to recognise the importance of mental training and struggle to understand how the mind works. Consequently, many of them tend to hide behind the ludicrous idea that you're either born with mental strength or you'll never have it. In fact, mental strength can be manufactured and built up in any willing athlete until they are positively overflowing with confidence, belief and winning feelings. It is the great broken link that any athlete must fix without delay if they wish to stay in contention with their more progressive rivals and it is exactly what the methods set out here are designed for - the opportunity to be truly in the zone and experience that beautiful state at will. The optimum state for competition is to be nice and relaxed with the correct amount of positive tension which is a kind of excitement. When you achieve the correct balance you enter what is known as the zone or the flow if you're a writer or the groove if you're a musician. And by the way, as I keep stressing, the same goes for whatever walk of life you happen to be involved in. These methods will work for you whatever you want to achieve. You can be in the zone stacking shelves in a supermarket, driving a truck or working as a bricklayer on a building site. It makes absolutely no difference. When you're in the zone you switch over to auto-pilot and your mind and body click into harmony. Everything is right, everything is perfect and you achieve remarkable results. Everything flows easily and effortlessly and you feel a surge of purpose and strength. You feel amazing and at that fantastic moment your performance skyrockets and you go further than you have ever gone before. That is what these methods do for you. Not only do they improve the athlete's performance level and help them achieve their full potential but it is absolutely certain that they cannot achieve their full potential without them. You don't get this kind of boost even with the best silk underwear. And it's the same whatever your job or profession. Promise

Exercise 16 - Affirmations

An affirmation is a strongly-worded, emotive sentence or phrase that you repeat to yourself as often as possible and is a device for keeping your self-talk positive and strong. For example, good affirmations are: I'm a winner - I can succeed, I will succeed - I can win, I will win - I'm a non-smoker, I'm losing weight easily and effortlessly, - I can make it - I can do this, I feel strong, confident and powerful etc. etc. In sport, business, show business and life generally you can invent your own affirmations that are most suitable for your situation. Just make sure they're positive and strong and mean something to you. You can change them either daily or weekly according to circumstances - when I get in front, I stay in front, I can do better, I'm calm and relaxed and totally in control and so on. I am a non-smoker. I am a clean air breather. I can lose weight easily and effortlessly. Fatty foods are of no interest to me. I enjoy healthy food. I prefer healthy food. I love green vegetables. This is another example of a very simple exercise that anyone can do anywhere and at any time. You don't need to say affirmations out loud. You can say them to yourself. Doesn't cost anything, doesn't take up too much time, doesn't require you to exert yourself in any way but the effect is amazing. Keeps the mind nice and strong. The more you follow this advice and carry out these things, the more positive thoughts will pass along neural pathways into the sub-conscious mind, the more the sub-conscious mind will believe them and the more they will be true. In turn, the more they will add just that little extra to your confidence, motivation, belief, performance etc. and one day it might be that little extra that wins the final point of a grand slam final or the winning goal in the cup final or gets you that job of a lifetime or that crucial contract you dreamed of or whatever else populates your list of aims and ambitions.

Crucial Moments

'Golf is ninety percent mental.' - Jack Nicklaus

Top professionals in any field are under intense pressure to succeed and at crucial moments of competition this often creates a physiological reaction causing muscles to tighten up. We've all seen the tennis player who plays beautifully to reach match point but then can hardly then get the ball over the net or the footballer who misses a penalty at a crucial time, a task he performs successfully almost every time in training. We've all heard about the Chief Executive who freezes at the point of delivering the big speech or the prize-winning author with writers' cramp or the experienced performer who gets stage fright. There are thousands of people like this. I know it well because they come to me for help. In their minds when they turn up it is an insoluble problem but an hour later it's gone!

At the British Open Golf Championship 2009 the 59-year old Tom Watson played beautifully and led the field for four days until he arrived at the final hole needing to sink a putt of intermediate difficulty to win the tournament and become the oldest major champion in golfing history. A putt that's normally easy for him. But these were not easy circumstances even for this most experienced of golfers. He missed and went on to lose the play-off to Stewart Clink in what was his only major championship win. What happens at moments like this is that the imminent point of winning creates a moment of intense anxiety and doubt in the mind causing muscles to tighten up with negative tension. At such a point the critical, conscious mind is butting in and saying things like 'What if I miss it?' 'What if I don't make it?' 'Maybe the other guy will get back into the match.' 'Maybe the momentum is turning in his favour.' 'I'm too old to win this.' 'I can't do it.' Etc. etc. So a positive situation is turned into a negative one by negative self-talk leading to a sudden loss of mental strength and belief.

What the player needs here is a performance trigger to help him relax and provide a boost of confidence, motivation, focus and belief so that he replaces the negative voice in his mind with a positive one saying 'I can do it and I will do it.' 'I've played well to get here and I can continue playing well.' 'The next point is just another point, just another day at the office' 'I've won many points in this match and I can win the next one.' Or 'I can make this.' Or 'I'm a winner.' Of course, anyone who works with me will have prepared mentally for this situation and so the mind will automatically switch into the positive mode required here. Any one of a number of performance triggers can instantly jog the mind into the correct focus when it is needed. In the heat of competition what has happened before doesn't concern you at all. The only thing that matters is what you do now. There are various performance trigger methods in this book so if you read it all you'll have them. It's a familiar scenario to many, particularly I suggest in the UK. Achieving a winning position and not being able to get over the finishing line. At such a moment the player needs to relax because when you relax your mind you relax your body. The mind and body are inextricably intertwined and inseparable. They have a mutual physiological interaction and that is one of the key reasons to train the mind with the kind of methods presented here to be able to deal with such a situation easily, effortlessly and automatically. The mind remembers states and when properly trained we can switch mental states easily. When annoying things happen you can get angry very quickly. In the same way with learned techniques you can, in the heat of competition, or at any other time you need, induce a calm state just as quickly. Tom Watson's putt would probably have gone in every time in a practice session so if he could have induced the relaxed mental state of the practice ground that putt might very well have sunk straight into the cup with the very satisfying clattering sound that all golfers love and in doing so created a major historical moment on that final hole of competition. Indeed, the historical significance of the moment probably stoked his anxiety.

Tapping the Healer Within
(With respect for the work of Dr. Roger Callahan.)

'I have no special talent. I am only passionately curious.' - Albert Einstein

Tapping is a modality whereby you tap on parts of your body and it changes your mental state. The points you tap are along the lines of the body's meridian energy system and they are the same as acupuncture points. The meridian energy system was discovered by Chinese doctors thousands of years ago and they were able to map its course through the body. Where it comes close to the surface of the skin are the points we tap and at the same time we do a few other things such as eye movements, counting and humming.

The pioneer of tapping in America was Dr. Roger Callahan who invented a modality called Thought Field Therapy (TFT). Then along came Gary Craig and developed it in a slightly different way and called his version Emotional Freedom Technique (EFT). There are now various tapping modalities which are mostly quite similar and all using the same terminology which I use here.

When I first heard about tapping I thought it sounded daft. I mean really, how can tapping with your fingertips on different parts of your body change anything at all? But I kept hearing about it from various sources and eventually even from people who I quite admired. So obviously I had to check it out. Why wouldn't I? After all for years I'd made a point of charging off to all kinds off far flung corners of the world to check out any crazy sounding modality I became aware of. Indeed, for many years I had been in the process of collecting any rapid, potent method I could find to add to my ever growing tool box of effective techniques. I still am. Actually, I tend to call it my toy box because it is always such great fun to show people these methods and watch the incredulity on their faces when they feel positive changes happening and realise that these methods do in fact work incredibly well. That they had been released from a lifetime of fear, phobia or trauma or quit a habit or got rid of crippling stress in about five minutes. This was a long time ago now and the stories of almost miraculous rapid healing using tapping grow by the day. Looking online you find countless similar stories to my own of wonderful results brought about by this magical modality. Of course this is not enough to persuade the hierarchy of the UK health authorities who dismiss all anecdotal evidence and require cast-iron, empirical proof of efficacy. As with most psych-sensory methods, there are few if any clinical trials to validate the enthusiasm of the thousands of practitioners around the world who produce amazing results with these methods. There is, however, a huge body of anecdotal proof all over the internet from all over the world citing successful case histories of many different kinds. The evidence is compelling, overwhelming and true. These methods work extremely well particularly in those areas where doctors struggle such as smoking, weight, stress, anxiety, depression, chronic fatigue and that old chestnut that is named after a description of its own symptoms, irritable bowel syndrome or IBS as it is more affectionately known. Sounds daft eh? But you know what? It's magical!

Map of tapping points

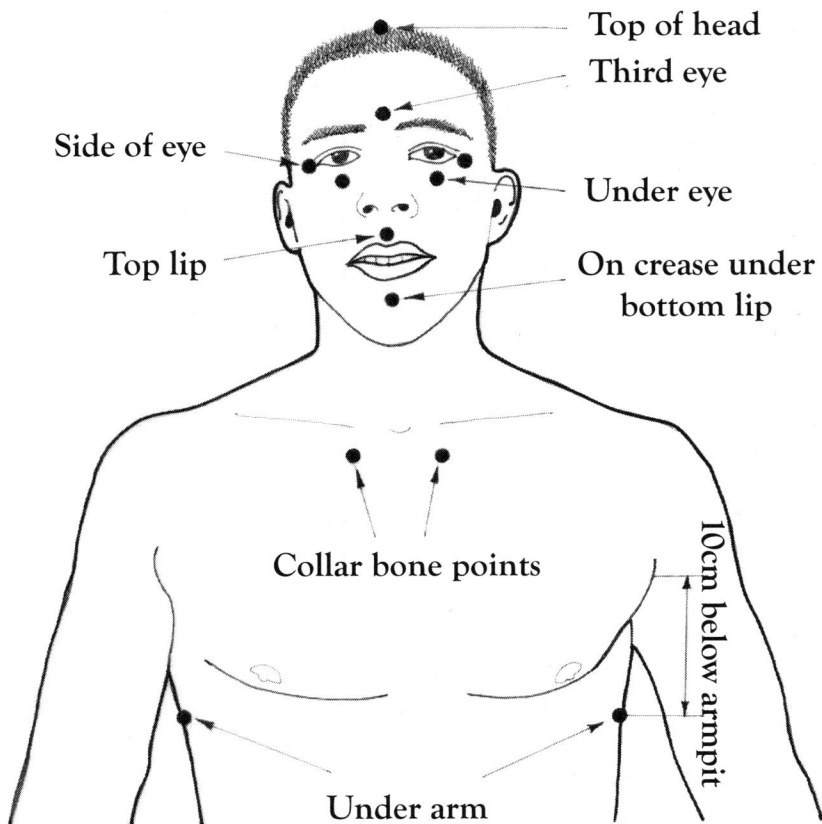

Top of head

Third eye

Side of eye

Under eye

Top lip

On crease under
bottom lip

Collar bone points

10cm below armpit

Under arm

Exercise 17 - The very Subtle Art of Finger Squeezing

From the Indian Mudras to Japanese Jin Shin Jyutsu to Acupressure derived from Chinese meridian therapy, pulling, tapping and squeezing fingers is a time-honoured yet relatively unknown method of healing physical and mental disorders. This is not a text book about any particular therapy but a selection of the various modalities I have studied and now use in my practice designed to encourage readers to investigate further. So to whet your appetite and get you started with this magical modality here now is a map with some basic finger tapping/squeezing points with their applications as directed by different finger tapping methods. It never ceases to amaze me how incredibly quick and effective these simple techniques can be and I really hope you are amazed too.

Sadness, grief, relationship, breathing

Panic, indecision, fatigue

Anger, frustration

Fear, digestion, back problems

Worry, stress, tension

Gamut spot

Lung Meridian (tap for increased lung capacity)

The karate point

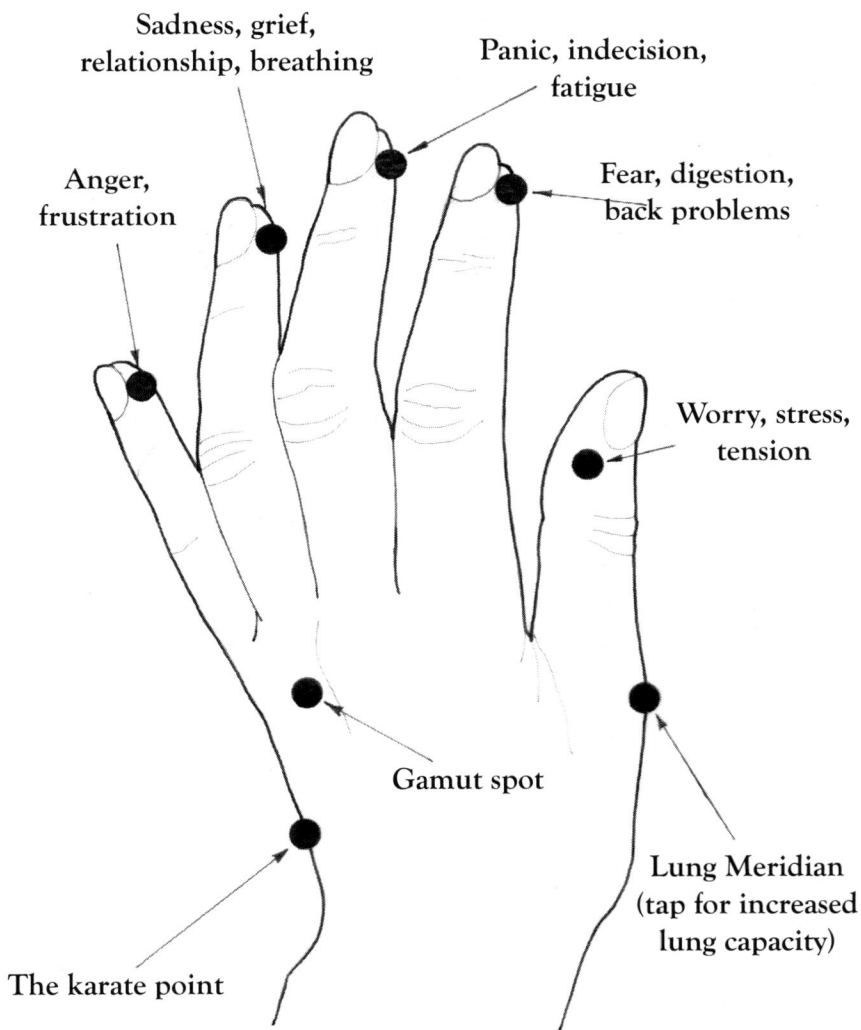

Finger tapping points and their use

What is Love?

'One thing we can never get enough of is love.' - Henry Miller

In the groups I am invited to work with there is often a cynic who does their best to challenge my assertions and prove me wrong particularly in regard to hypnosis but also with the other modalities I demonstrate and wholeheartedly recommend. They might say there's no proof that any of it works, that it's a placebo, that it doesn't exist etc. etc. Once at a teachers' convention in London a particularly disaffected member of my audience, a rather large, red-faced, heavily-bearded individual, waded in almost as soon as I started. Without a by your leave he sounded off at me saying hypnosis was not scientific, that I couldn't prove it was true, that it was all just a scam etc. etc. and waited for my response. All eyes were on me and I could tell people were embarrassed that this guy had put me on the spot so early in the piece. So I asked him whether he knew that Einstein used hypnosis and had discovered the theory of relativity whilst in a hypnotic trance. I guess he didn't because he piped down after that and seemed to enjoy the rest of my presentation. Afterwards, people came up and apologised for his behaviour. Turns out they were used to it because my heckler was head of the science faculty and well known for taking to task anything he considered unscientific. In a lot of cases these cynical types are doctors who prefer to prescribe medicine with an active ingredient they know will work. Or does it? In most cases it's nothing more than guesswork. With mental illness it's a trial and error process and psychiatrists might prescribe a number of potions before finding one that has the effect they are looking for which is basically to balance up chemicals in the brain such as serotonin, oxytocin, dopamine etc. and quell the erratic behaviour of their client. The actual effect in most cases of people taking these psychotropic drugs is that they become totally subdued and shadows of their former selves. In other words they become virtual zombies for lack of any other suitable word. They still have the problem but they just don't care about it anymore. They can't be bothered to be bothered about being bothered. In my experience, athletes who are prescribed drugs like these tend to lose their ambition and are happy to jog along at whatever level they've already reached. This is the complete opposite of the mind-set of most serious athletes who are determined at all times to reach the highest possible performance level.

Recently it was discovered that if you administered a placebo and actually told the patient it was a placebo it still worked. How scientific is that by the way? People get used to taking pills and other medicines and doctors are used to prescribing them without even bothering to give a single thought to the fact that there are simple, rapid, holistic methods for achieving the same outcome without ingesting chemicals. Actually they don't even know these methods exist. They simply fail to understand or even try to understand how the mind works and that it is an incredibly powerful tool, more powerful than any computer, providing us all with the innate ability to heal ourselves. Even raising these matters directly with doctors merely elicits some vague acknowledgement such as 'Oh really, that's interesting'. Without actually trying to absorb the subject matter. They simply ignore the whole issue. They are conditioned so to do. They can't see it so it doesn't exist. It's like a small child who covers their eyes with their hands and thinks you have disappeared. When we're born we are bestowed with this amazingly powerful instrument, the kneck-top computer or brain as we normally refer to it, but we don't get an instruction manual to show us how to use it properly. Because of this when it makes mistakes as it frequently does we don't know how to fix it and we tend to compound the issue by fiddling around with the wrong elements. So consider this if you will. We flick a switch and the light comes on. The light is powered by electricity. This is something we all believe in. The electricity that powers lights and radios and televisions and washing machines and computers and all the various gadgets that are pretty much essential to modern day living. We know it exists and we benefit enormously from its power and woe-betide anyone who doesn't pay their electricity bill because the company that provides it will take it away. We flick a switch and we absolutely expect the light to come on. We all do. We have to have it. We can't do without it. So tell me then, what does it look like? Yes that's right, what does electricity look like? You can't see it but you use it every day, you believe in it, you know it's there and you expect it to work every time but can you describe it? Think of someone you love or maybe some people you love. This is what makes life worth living more than anything else isn't it? Certainly all the major philosophers agree that the only thing in life that has any real value is love. I agree with that. We are literally prepared to die for the people we love. If your wife and kids were in danger of their lives most of us would willingly change places with them so they could survive over ourselves. I would. This is the power of love. The most powerful of all emotions. We all want to be in love. We enjoy being in love. We like hearing songs about love. We like poems about love. We like films about love. We like reading books about love. We love to love. We want to fall in love. Love at first sight. The very fabric of our existence is interwoven with love. So please tell me if you will, what does it look like? Can you prove it exists? Where does it come from? Where does it live? How do you get it? Can I have a prescription for it please? As I have already mentioned, I've worked with some high-achieving athletes, artists and business folk at times when they reached the height of their powers but I can't prove their success had anything to do with me or my methods. But they know. They know how they felt after sessions and when performing and they know how they were able to experience a positive shift in their mental powers when I worked with them. They can't see it but they know it exists. Same as love. And electricity.

Anchors and Triggers

'Confidence works wonders sometimes.' - Roger Federer

As we already know, the mind remembers states. If you anchor a state in your mind such as the way you felt when you performed very well and achieved something significant, that made you feel happy, proud and successful, then you can trigger that anchor at any time you want so that you feel the same way again and perform the same way again.

If you anchor your mind to the way you felt when you were the most relaxed you've ever been in your life you can trigger that feeling when you have to give that awkward presentation, when you walk on the stage to appear with your band at the Albert Hall, at match point in the final of a tennis grand-slam tournament or at a penalty shoot-out in the football World Cup Final or at the last hole and final putt of the British Open Golf Tournament in front of a world-wide audience of millions and all you'll need to worry about is which room to keep the trophy in.

Anchoring is a simple process and there are many ways of doing it that are demonstrated and taught in my events and workshops. You can observe top players and athletes triggering anchors by taking big deep breaths before serving, driving, putting, on the blocks, taking free kicks etc. Pumping fists, reaching for the towel, holding fingers together etc. There's a tried and tested performance trigger methods in these pages. Learn it and use it and you'll find it useful for the rest of your life whatever you are doing. Not just in sport but every aspect of existence.

Indeed, here it is now.

Exercise 18 - Performance Trigger or Rapid Confidence Boost

Recommended any time you need a boost of positive feelings or performance enhancement.

Remember a time when you felt really great. The best you ever felt in your life. It could be a time when you achieved or won something. When you performed well in sport or on the stage, passed an exam, landed a great job, found a great partner, signed a big deal, fell in love, fulfilled something from your bucket list. Maybe your wedding day or when your kids were born. These are just suggestions but pick out your own great memory of a time when you felt positive, loving, joyful feelings flowing through your mind and body. Place the thumb and middle finger of your dominant hand together. Close your eyes, drift back through time into that special moment and be there now. Experience vividly everything about it. See what you saw, hear what you heard, feel what you felt. See the other people who were there. Was it inside or outside? Feel the temperature. Feel everything else about that great moment when you felt the best you ever felt. As you remember that moment so vividly, press that thumb and finger together a little stronger and feel all those great feelings you had at that time flooding back through your body a little stronger. All those wonderful, winning, loving, positive, joyful feelings. Feel them all flooding back through your body and know that at any time in the future, if you're competing in sport or business or striving for a great performance level in any other area of life and need a boost. If you're feeling a little low and need a lift. Whatever you need and whenever you need it all you need to do is place that thumb and finger together and instantly feel all those strong, confident, winning, loving, positive feelings flooding back through your body enabling you to feel just like you did when you felt at your best and allowing you to perform at your best level, at the height of your powers. The level you performed when you were at your very best. Open your eyes. Feel great.

Superhuman Effort

'I could be bounded in a nutshell, and count myself a king of infinite space, were it not that I have bad dreams.' - William Shakespeare

At the 2010 Wimbledon Tennis championships John Isner of the USA and Nicolas Mahut of France, both excellent and very experienced tennis players, sauntered out into the warmth of a sunny court eighteen to begin their first round match. Three days later they were still playing. It took eleven hours and five minutes of what turned out to be the longest match in tennis history to separate the two players and come up with a winner. In a contest dominated largely by serve, momentum switched back and forth with hardly an error being made by either player. Eventually, after a superhuman effort by both of these modern day gladiators, John Isner emerged victorious winning the last set by a gargantuan seventy games to sixty-eight! The slightest of margins in a massive score. Isner was so hungry at the conclusion he said he could eat twelve big Macs! The final score was 6-4, 3-6, 6-7(7-9), 7-6(7-3), 70-68. A total of 183 games. At the conclusion, both players had broken numerous records including that both had served over one hundred aces in what became known as 'The endless match'.

The final set alone which lasted eight hours and eleven minutes was by itself longer than the whole of the previous longest match at the 2004 French Open between Fabrice Santoro and Arnaud Clement which had lasted merely six hours and thirty-three minutes.

The chair umpire of this record-breaking contest, Swedish official Mohamed Lahyani, also rose to the occasion on the day saying afterwards he was so gripped by the amazing match that his concentration stayed solid and he did not even think about eating or going to the toilet.

Even the scoreboard malfunctioned because it was not programmed for so many games. At fifty - fifty in the final set it had to be reset to nil, nil and spectators were asked to 'please add fifty to the game score'.

Many observers and TV pundits commented at the time that it was a shame there could only be one winner and indeed this would be very salient statement were it not for the most fundamental and cogent fact that winning is the entire purpose of the activity.

As it happens, I was at Wimbledon on the middle day of that match and stopped by court eighteen for about ten minutes on my way somewhere else. It was easy to find a seat in the shade close to the action and eat my sandwich while leisurely taking in the sport. Of course, this was before things had turned into a marathon and little did I realise that I was witnessing ten minutes of tennis history. Later that day as word spread around the grounds about the unfolding drama on court eighteen a huge crowd gathered with hundreds of spectators crushing in to any nook and cranny, vying for a decent vantage point and straining every sinew to get a glimpse of the action.

Such was the excitement generated by this extraordinary contest both in the grounds and on nationwide television that at its conclusion the All England Club, represented on this occasion by Britain's finest semi-finalist Tim Henman, presented both players and the umpire with a crystal bowl and champagne flutes. Something never to happen either before or since.

The point about this of course is that on that particular day those two amazing players raised their performance levels beyond anything previously known and broke new boundaries in grit, determination, endurance and skill. They demonstrated very clearly that there is another level, a better, higher level of mental toughness that it is possible for anyone to achieve. They were good players but not the best players. Together they found resources of energy, endurance and resilience far beyond the normal. Together they pushed each other through walls no one had ever been through. They reached new levels that had not been known. A glimpse of the promised land! This is similar in some ways to the Roger Bannister story earlier in the book and poses an obvious choice for anyone who wishes to make the best of themselves whether they are international tennis players or any other type of athlete, business people, artists of any kind, bricklayers, cooks, truck drivers or anyone else at all in any walk of life.

Do we languish in our comfort zone and settle for the limiting beliefs created by others or do we throw caution to the wind and strive to achieve great things, break records, go further, shrug off worry, doubt and fear so that we can turn on the world with our skill, beauty and excellence? Unequivocally, the methods and techniques I present here are designed to achieve the latter. Smash through those mental barriers and let's see what's on the other side!

By the way, at the 2018 Wimbledon Championships John Isner reached the semi-final where he played against Kevin Anderson in a match that turned out to be the second longest ever at six and a half hours with the score in the final set 26-24. So Isner has the distinction of playing in both the longest and second longest matches in history. But these long matches are not liked by the authorities, the public or the players and ways are afoot to prevent it happening again. The authorities have problems with scheduling when a match takes so long, the public has a problem getting home late with a sore backside and the players are so exhausted that the winner cannot recover quickly enough and loses badly in the next round. They are talking about bringing in a last set tie break for grand slam matches so this never happens again but my suggestion is much easier. Don't allow John Isner to enter the competition!

Fabrice Moamba

Have a heart

It is 17th March 2012 and at a packed White Hart Lane heaving with excitement the teams ran out on to the pitch for this FA Cup Quarter final tie between Tottenham Hotspur and Bolton Wanderers. Fourty-one minutes into the game the Bolton player Fabrice Moamba collapsed on the pitch with no other player near him. This immediately alarmed Bolton physiotherapist Andy Mitchell. 'He went down in a sort of slow-motion, face forward way which was completely not right.' He recalls. 'My instincts were telling me something was seriously wrong here.' Andy didn't wait for the referee's permission to enter the pitch as the rules dictate. He just went on.

Medics of both clubs also raced onto the pitch including a consultant cardiologist who was at the game as a fan. All the players gathered round with concerned expressions. The crowd hushed itself into silence realising something serious was afoot. Millions of television viewers around the country were gripped with tension as doctors administered defibrillator shocks and Fabrice was transferred to an ambulance. Referee Howard Webb abandoned the match. The world of football waited and worried.

Later it transpired that Fabrice had suffered a cardiac arrest and to all intents and purposes was dead for 78 minutes. But to the great joy of all concerned and those football fans around the globe who were caught up in the drama, Fabrice Moamba survived. Two weeks after the incident a photograph was released of Fabrice sitting up in his hospital bed and smiling. Doctors described it as a miracle that he was alive. Since then Fabrice and his partner Shauna have had a baby and Fabrice has graduated with honours from university.

But what exactly happened here? My theory is as follows.

They don't know why Fabrice collapsed. Doctors are unable to provide the answer to this. A common cause of similar incidents is hypertrophic cardiomyopathy which is a thickening of the heart muscle and since Moamba's scare more than a dozen professional footballers have died from it. It is very hard to diagnose and impossible now to tell if that is what happened to Fabrice because his heart has undergone too many changes since. There can be no doubt that the brilliant care Fabrice received as he lay on the field by those excellent doctors who happened to be present was a major factor in his survival. But whatever the medical explanations I believe another major factor in this extraordinary event was the positive energy of everyone in the ground and all those listening on the radio and the millions watching on TV which helped Fabrice to be okay. Everyone wanted him to be okay and willed him to be okay and the combined sum total of all that incredible, positive energy flowing towards him helped to keep him alive. As human beings we can do this. So let's think about this energy and think about what we have done with this energy and think about what wonderful things we can make happen in the future by using this energy in the most positive way we can.

Marrakesh Success

'Never make a single move without first visualising a successful outcome.' - *Jack Nicklaus*

We were sitting by the pool in a country in North Africa. Morocco to be factual and Marrakesh to be precise. But it could have been anywhere. South of France, Umbria, Canaries, the Algarve, Costa del Sol. The folks all packed in on loungers around the water were mostly Brits smoking, drinking, eating pizza, talking rubbish. Like I say, could have been anywhere that Ryanair goes.

Three young people, a girl and two boys, probably about in their mid-twenties were taking it in turns to swim a length of the pool underwater but without success. After a couple of tries the first boy succeeded and embarked on a ritual of celebration worthy of a premiership footballer scoring a goal in the cup final. Whooping, jumping, high-fiving anyone in the vicinity. But the girl seemed exasperated. 'I can't do this' She said before pushing off under the water, propelling herself about half way and then re-emerging, coughing, spitting, burping and swearing. 'Fuck.' She said. The second lad tried again but emerged about five yards short. The first lad, knackered by his exertions, had now retired to his lounger and sat watching the others in action, sipping a beer and basking in the glow of his success. His work here was done. Now the girl was ready to try again. 'I'll never do it' she declared before gliding beneath the surface and pushing off towards her distant target. My beloved and I had been following all these antics with great interest from the comfort of our loungers on the other side of the pool and were fascinated by the interplay between these young folk. 'She won't do it if she says things like that.' I pronounced. And indeed, perhaps a little further this time but still no cigar. The second boy now pushed off with great determination and gets closer, closer, closer, yes! Done it!. Cue wild celebrations and whoops of delight. But the girl looked on with a sullen demeanour. 'Fuck.' She said. Clearly a young lady of few words. But this time she slid into position with a more determined expression almost like an Olympic athlete going for a world record. 'I'm going to do it this time.' She announced. More to herself than anyone else. But we heard her. 'Just watch now.' I said in my usual, pompous manner. 'Bet she'll do it this time.' And guess what, she did! It was about the most perfect example of positive self-talk you could possibly imagine played out right in front of us. I couldn't have contrived it better if I had written the script, hired the actors and filmed it in Hollywood. And before you ask, yes this is entirely true and, by the way, the same goes for everything else in this book. There may be a few flights of fancy here and there but nothing to misguide or mislead. Only to help. When the girl in the pool said she couldn't do it she failed in the task but the moment she told herself she could do it, she succeeded. So let it be a lesson to us all. Out of the mouths of babes etc. etc. It is the kind of approach I prattle on about all the time because it's incredibly simple yet incredibly important and applicable to every area of life. If you believe you can do something you have a chance of doing it. If you don't believe you can do it you probably won't. Therefore, my advice to everyone who wishes to do things, to succeed with things, to achieve things, is to practise believing. All the exercises in this book are specifically designed to help you do exactly that. Here, carried out by complete amateurs larking about in a hotel swimming pool in Marrakesh was the perfect example of a basic truth of which ambitious folk in all fields would do well to take note. How I wish I could have filmed it to play to my clients or at my workshops.

Mental Strength

'There are more things in heaven and earth, Horatio, than are dreamt of in your philosophy.' - William Shakespeare - Hamlet

So what is mental strength? Where does it come from? How do you get it? Why is it that some athletes, actors, entertainers, speakers, executives etc. perform at a consistently high level in training, practice or rehearsal but cannot reproduce the same standard in matches, when the audience is present or in an exam? These are questions that mystify players, athletes, coaching professionals, teachers and others involved (particularly TV pundits) but the answers are actually quite simple and for the benefit of any doubt, here they are:

Mental strength is a mix of four ingredients - confidence, belief, motivation and focus.

It comes from inside you.

You get it by following the mental training guidelines set out in these pages, by participating in my workshops and by having sessions with me. By the way, this is my definition. You won't find it in any psychology text book but you never know, maybe some psychologists will agree with me about this.

Please listen carefully. If you carry out the methods I set out here, and they are not difficult, you will raise your performance level whatever you're doing without any doubt whatsoever because this is scientific and always works. Very often the effect is rapid and dramatic and sometimes it is more subtle but there is always a significant improvement right from the start. It doesn't necessarily mean you'll be perfect and win every time but it does mean you'll have a better chance of being perfect and winning every time. What's it all about Alfie? Inspired performance. World-class performance. World-class happiness. That's what it's all about Alfie.

Exercise 19 - Future Pacing

The Picture in Your Palm

Stand up straight with your feet slightly apart.

Hold your arm up above your head with your open palm facing down at you.

Look up into your palm and imagine things exactly the way you want them to be assuming everything is perfect. Make the image compelling and powerful. Make it colourful and joyful.

Now double the intensity of the picture in your palm and make it twice as bright.

Imagine beautiful music playing through it.

Now double the intensity again. Feel everything becoming twice as powerful. And now make everything ten times more intense again. Make it ten times brighter and the emotion ten times stronger. Those positive feelings ten times more powerful. The music ten times more hypnotic.

Feel those amazing feelings flooding through your body and mind. And now increase the intensity by a thousand times. Make it a thousand times more powerful.

And now, when it all looks and feels amazing. When it is absolutely perfect. When it is exactly the way you want it to be and only then.........

Take a nice, big deep breath in and then as you breathe out pull that picture into your chest and absorb it right in through your heart. Rub it into your torso, spread it around and feel all those wonderful feelings being absorbed into your being.

Then take another nice, big deep breath in and as you breathe in intensify the image again, multiply it by one thousand times and as you breathe out spread that intense, powerful, bright and colourful feeling right through your whole body into every muscle, nerve, fibre and tissue until you feel completely saturated with wonderful feelings. Feel great and full of love. Use it as much as you like.

Future pacing

We Can't All Be Right (or left)

'Throughout history, it has been the inaction of those who could have acted; the indifference of those who should have known better; the silence of the voice of justice when it mattered most; that has made it possible for evil to triumph.' - Haile Selassie

There's a scene in the famous musical Fiddler on the Roof where Tevya the milkman is discussing matters with two of his friends who are in dispute with each other. A crowd has gathered round to watch. The first states his case about the issue in question and Tevya says 'Yes, you're right.'

The second then puts the opposite opinion forward and Tevya says 'Yes you're also right.'

A third person who is listening to the debate says 'Tevya, you say he's right and he is also right. But they can't both be right'. To which Tevya answers 'Yes you're right too.'

Now not only is this a brilliant dialogue conceived by the wonderful Yiddish writer Sholem Aleichem who wrote the original 'Tevya the Milkman' from which Fiddler is derived but it is also an excellent guide to negotiating strategy for this reason. If we are prepared to accept that the other side in an argument is right rather than insisting the other side is completely, utterly and very badly wrong then we have a much better chance of reaching agreement even to some of the most intractable issues of the day.

You see it works like this and in my opinion it is incredibly important that we all make an effort to understand what I am about to say because if we do we may be able to appreciate and even love each other a bit more. Oh, and we may be able to put an end to war as well.

We each have our own internal representation of the world which means that we all perceive things differently. So what you see is not necessarily what I see even if we are looking at the very same thing. The same goes for concepts and ideas. Our minds interpret them differently. Therefore, no matter how logical something may seem to you it is very possible that the self-same thing may seem totally illogical to me. Not because I am trying to be difficult but because I genuinely perceive it differently to you because my brain interprets it differently to your brain due to a number of factors such as conditioning, age, experience, gender, nationality, ethnicity and, probably the most influential although we can't be sure, paleo-ancestral memory. For this reason, as an example, cross-generational communication doesn't work. The teenager who comes home in the early hours after having harmless fun with his mates does not perceive he is doing anything wrong but the parents who have been waiting up and worrying their heads off all night getting angrier as the hours passed by think their son is either thoroughly inconsiderate and totally beyond redemption or that some terrible fate has befallen him.

The parents of course completely forget that they used to behave in a similar way when they were the same age but that is forgotten because everything is relative and they have since quelled the rebellion that used to make them behave like their son partly indeed by the very act of conceiving him in the first place. Right now though they feel like they feel and it's almost unbearable.

The Muslim who wishes to establish a state based on Sharia law because he thinks it's the way God wishes us to behave and sees western values as immoral cannot possibly find it in his heart to agree with the Catholic who lives next door who wishes to evict Muslims from the country (or at least the street) because he thinks they don't understand the proper Christian values that God wishes us to follow and sees Sharia law as dangerous and immoral.

Yes, I know, there's a very good case for saying they are both wrong but these are deeply engrained and very passionate beliefs and you can't just dismiss them as rubbish even if that's what you think because it will end in a fight and if you fight them they will fight you back. Bingo! There you have it. A lifelong, intractable dispute that enrages everybody and ends in a vicious cycle of tragic violence fomented by the extremists on both sides who are not prepared to even listen to the other viewpoint let alone accept it. A knife can be used to cut bread or stab someone.

What is to be done? It may go against the grain and seem difficult at first but once you get the hang of it becomes incredibly easy. Try this. Accept that the other side may be right and use that as a sounding off point for discussions. Accept that the other side sincerely believes that they are right even though you completely disagree with them. Then what you may find is that your opponents will listen to what you have to say with an element of respect and accept that you too believe you are right. It is pointless continuing to insist the other side is wrong. They just see it differently to you and vice versa. They feel they are right and you feel you are right. So that's it then. You are both right. Accept the other side is right. Allow them to accept that you are right and rejoice. There is nothing to fight about any more. Mutual respect is what's needed. Isolate the extremists.

My father once said be gentle with each other during a period when my wife and I didn't see eye to eye. It was the best advice I ever received and I pass it on to you now. To that I will add the following - Love each other as much as possible because we are all brothers and sisters.

Triple Whammy - Proof of the Pudding

'You can't turn the clock back and change what happened however much you may want to.' - Peter Gilmour

Throughout the pages of this book I continually stress the efficacy of the methods I'm writing about to the point where it might even be to the annoyance of the reader. But there is a very good reason for this which is that I have absolute proof of what I am saying. This chapter explains it.

People seem to want cast-iron, empirical evidence for everything these days because to a large extent we have lost contact with the basic instincts by which we can know what is good for us and what isn't. My experience tells me that most people have never heard about the kind of methods I write about here and will most likely be influenced by the plethora of sceptics persuading them these kind of things are all rubbish. Accordingly, they find the concept of complementary therapies hard to assimilate and need the comfort of scientific proof before they will take it seriously. But this approach is hardly consistent. Do those same people for instance need the same proof for the existence of love? Most of us believe it's best thing available in life and seek it avidly yet who can prove it exists? Where's the scientific proof? Of course, I doubt if many sceptics are reading this thing anyway but for those who are I will explain very clearly not just how I know these methods and techniques work but how I am absolutely one hundred percent certain they do. Furthermore, as I have said elsewhere, even though there may not be much empirical evidence available there is a wealth of anecdotal evidence everywhere you look bearing testimony to the wonderful efficacy of these kind of techniques. Incidentally, the reason for the dearth of empirical testing for complementary methods is partly because of the holistic culture of the approach albeit there have been quite a number of experiments such as for instance inserting acupuncture needles into a subject in an MRI scanner and recording the surrounding area explode with energy and light.

But it is also because these trials are incredibly expensive and only pharmaceutical companies, which are amongst the wealthiest and most powerful of all commercial entities, can afford it. They are able to allocate huge funds towards any research that will attest to the efficacy of the products they market on a worldwide basis even if the research is not always entirely correct. For instance for years they promoted thalidomide as a safe drug against morning sickness in pregnant women many of whom gave birth to severely deformed children as a result. It was a scandal that caused widespread grief and unhappiness and those companies had to be dragged kicking and screaming though the courts for many years before paying compensation for the suffering they caused. Tobacco companies promoted smoking cigarettes as a healthy pastime for many years. The current rise in the use of opioids in the UK with its associated horror stories is another developing pharma scandal.

The thousands of amazing case studies concerning energy medicine you can find on the internet are very similar to my own amazing cases but having said that, I stress that this particular chapter is not about the many hundreds of clients I or anyone else has successfully treated even they do augment the evidence. No, this chapter is entirely about my own experiences. At the beginning of 2004 I had a decent, comfortable and happy life but by the end of it everything had totally collapsed on all fronts. Love, health and finances. An uncontrollable triple whammy. People who hear the story often comment they're surprised I'm still standing. At that time Lesley and I had been together since 1976, through thick and thin as they say. Twenty-eight mostly happy years, two wonderful kids, a great house, villa in

Spain, nice cars, profitable family business, close friends (or so I thought). We travelled abroad regularly, went to nice restaurants, visited cultural centres around the UK and Europe for art shows, concerts, business shows, sports events etc. Made love more than most married couples as far as I can ascertain and felt pretty happy with each other and life generally. As far as thick and thin are concerned it was actually mostly thick. Then out of the blue my wife Lesley was diagnosed with breast cancer and had a mastectomy followed by a breast reconstruction in a combined operation that lasted about eight hours. Obviously it was a hammer blow to our existence. We had to close down the family business, a chain of small clothing stores, which Lesley ran, because she wasn't well enough to do it anymore whilst I continued with my writing and mental performance and hypnosis practice as much as I could in between tending to Lesley and looking after the kids etc. At the time they were young teenagers at school and needed a lot of ferrying around to their various activities plus of course there were the daily visits to Lesley in a hospital about an hours' drive away. I was also caring for my Dad who needed a lot of love and attention after we lost my Mum. He was in his nineties and had his own health issues in addition to the deep loneliness he felt without his devoted partner of sixty-six years.

But Lesley was determined to recover as fast as possible and never wanted people fussing around her much. Yes, one of those. At her insistence, two days after leaving hospital and with a massive, great fresh scar all the way down her front, round her side and across her back we went out to dinner with friends at a local restaurant. We took a big cushion for her to lean on.

So she was recovering very quickly but now I wasn't feeling at all well. I tried to ignore it and crack on regardless as guys often do but in the end I went to the doctor and described my symptoms to be told I had IBS (irritable bowel syndrome) and was prescribed tablets for it. I felt an uncomfortable ache deep in my gut and was in constant danger of being caught short but Paul the doctor (I knew him well) didn't think there was anything to worry about or that required urgent action. However, the tablets didn't work and I was feeling progressively worse. I now know most doctors would regard the symptoms I presented with as red flags for a man of my age yet even after a further few visits to the surgery my guy still wasn't too bothered about it. Eventually, after about five months of suffering, the condition was affecting my life so much that I became incensed enough to march into the surgery one bright and sunny day and almost bang my fist on the table to insist on some kind of action. Accordingly, the doctor referred me for a colonoscopy (reluctantly so it seemed at the time) but still didn't find it necessary to mark it urgent and so another six weeks went by before I turn up on the big day. The colorectal consultant who performed the magical mystery tour around my bowel was called Professor Brown would you believe. As I lay there grinning madly in a mild stupor from the effect of the sedatives pouring into my arm I could see the screen displaying the probing progress of the tiny yet powerful camera through my insides. An amazing and quite fascinating experience. The drugs made me light-headed and I was making jokes. 'Never had my own TV show before.' I said. Nobody laughed. I think they may have heard it before. Anyway, they seemed to be focussing on a shadowy protrusion appearing on the screen. Later, as I recovered with tea and regulation NHS digestive biscuits, Professor Brown popped in to discuss his findings.

'Yes we found the problem.' He announced cheerily.

'Oh good.' I said, matching his cheeriness.

'Yes, bit of a lump in there. Got to come out.' He announced and made his way towards the door. 'They'll make all the arrangements. Got to rush, bye.'

'Thanks again doc.' I said still affected by the weakening sedatives and perversely more interested in the biscuits than the diagnosis because they starve you before this procedure and I hadn't eaten for over twenty-four hours. They were the best biscuits I had ever tasted. But then my brain suddenly switched on and a bell rang in my head. Ding dong! By this time Professor Brown was halfway through the door and I had to muster all my energy to raise my voice enough to catch his attention.

'Hang on doctor.' I shouted. 'A lump? Did you say a lump? What sort of a lump?'

Realising his escape had been foiled he turned and approached my bed.

'That's it old boy. Bit of a tumour. Got to come out. Don't worry. They'll organise it all.'

'A tumour? You mean a malignant tumour?'

'Well we've taken a biopsy, the lab will tell us the result later'.

'So it's not sure yet?'

'Well not officially but I've seen enough of these to know what it is.'

'And you're sure it's a tumour?'

Yes, 'fraid so old boy. But they'll get it out. Happens all the time. Nothing to worry about.'

'Are you telling me it's cancer?'

'Yes, that's right old chap. But they'll sort it out. Well, got to rush, bye.' And he was gone.

So now, after six months of taking useless pills for IBS and being told there was nothing to worry about I was now being told I had bowel cancer. Now all of a sudden it was bloody well urgent. So that within a week or two they were slicing me right open and peering around every nook and cranny of my insides to find the diseased bit which was situated in my sigmoid colon. Probably the most inaccessible place in the whole body. However, I'm elated to report that the operation was a success and I'm perfectly okay now.

The surgeon told me he checked all my other organs on the way round. Liver, spleen, pancreas, the lot. But the outcome wasn't immediately quite that simple. After the operation a mistake in medication at the hospital caused an ulcer and I experienced excruciating pain at night for months before we found out what was happening. At first the doctors insisted it was post-operative 'settling down' and that I was being an over sensitive prima donna but it wasn't. They had forgotten to give me a drug to protect my stomach from the ant-inflammatory medication they'd prescribed which consequently burnt a hole in my stomach. The searing pain and sleepless nights went on for about four months. Lesley said she could see the pain in my face. Actually, she was the one who found out what was going on by searching the internet. When we realised what it was beyond any reasonable doubt we booked an appointment to see the doctor and told him that a number of websites indicated I might have an ulcer. 'Yes I thought it might be something like that'. He said. This after causing me pain and misery for four months. Anyway, I stopped taking all the pain killers and the pain went away. Amazing!

But those four months were very fateful for another reason because the very week I was diagnosed coincided exactly with the publication of my first novel 'Sexy Football' which was all printed up and sitting on the shelves waiting for the punters to rock up and buy it. I had been booked to speak at literary festivals around the country and appear on TV to promote it but of course I was simply not well enough to do any of that. What happens with books is that you have a window of about three months to publicise a new publication and then the publisher moves on to promote the next batch of new books coming out. So I missed the whole thing. I don't know if you realise how hard it is to get a book published in the mainstream as a debut novelist but it is actually almost impossible. I had done all the hard stuff, written the thing in the first place, found an agent, got a publisher and even received an advance against royalties. A miracle! Ask any author. But now I was stopped in my tracks by this damned disease. About four year's work up in smoke just like that. They say that guys never go to the doctor with this kind of thing and there are posters up all over doctors' surgeries urging men to seek advice if they develop the kind of symptoms I had. Well I was the one who did go and they missed it. After the operation, my very expert and wonderful colorectal surgeon Aiden Fowler told me that in the six months it took to diagnose me the tumour had 'popped out' of the bowel wall obviously making things more acute. Lesley and I had a healthy diet, didn't drink that much, exercised regularly and were happier than most so why did we get it?

I asked Aiden Fowler as he sat on my bed one day
'How did I get this thing?'
'You'll never know.' He replied.

Altogether it took about a year to recover and begin working to any proper extent again but I was highly motivated and completely devoted to the task so I was able to build up my practice again very quickly and get things back on track. Panic over.

However, two years after my bowel operation I somehow injured my back quite badly and found myself plumbing new depths in the experience of pain. I simply couldn't move in any direction without severe thunderclaps of agony in my back and legs. My local doctor, yes the same guy again, said it was probably sciatica and prescribed pain killers and physio treatment. But it didn't improve. In fact it got worse. The Physio sent me back to the doctor and he explained that he was an expert in muscular-skeletal matters and even gave lectures to other doctors on the subject so he knew what he was doing. The phrase 'blind leading the blind' eventually came to mind but I didn't know then what I know now. He stood steadfastly by his original diagnosis. It occurs to me that's what he always does regardless of any evidence to the contrary. Then one night I woke up with something called saddle anaesthesia which means that the whole of the middle part of your body becomes numb and I can assure you that it is a most frightening feeling. It was a different doctor who visited me at home to investigate this occurrence and he acted immediately wasting no time in organising an emergency appointment at the orthopaedic department of the local hospital. However, after many hours of waiting around in that very busy department and undergoing various tests, the consultant surgeon there backed up the original diagnosis (why shouldn't he? After all, my doctor was an expert in the subject) and told me to continue with the physio and pain relief. Once again however the physio was worried and sent me back to the doctor. At least someone knew what they were doing. To cut a long story short, about six months later, I found myself sitting in front of a different, more senior, orthopaedic consultant who told me that if I had seen him on that night I was first referred to the hospital he would have operated on me straight away and given me no choice in the matter. Furthermore, he told me it was only by a sheer stroke of luck I wasn't a paraplegic! If I had been standing up at that point I would definitely have collapsed because hearing this made me feel decidedly giddy. In total shock. Apparently, the condition I had was called cauda equine syndrome (literally, horse's tail) and it refers to the bundle of nerves that emanates from the end of the spine and connects up with everything in the lower body. Bowel function, bladder function, sexual function, all the motor functions, everything. I had a severe double prolapsed disc that was pressing on the cauda equine and when that happens all those functions can stop and never be re-enacted again. By the time I saw that second consultant, Bill Harcourt, a double first from Cambridge who actually did know what he was talking about, the main trauma had very luckily passed without those things happening but for your information dear reader, cauda equine syndrome often leads to catastrophic outcomes and is one of the main causes of huge litigation cases against health authorities. All my symptoms were bright, blood-red flags flapping wildly in the breeze but my doctor, the expert lecturer in muscular-skeletal matters, completely missed it. Generally speaking it is the consultants who have the expertise and take the risks and constantly increase their knowledge.

I had the spinal surgery and it took about half an hour followed by an overnight stay in hospital and have never had any back pain since. A few days later I was back at work but only part-time at first according to doctor's orders. Now our finances became difficult because neither of us could work properly and we started squabbling about money, then arguing a lot about everything else.

Then, lo and behold, I inadvertently discovered she was having an affair with a rather uninspiring sort of nitwit who not only worked for me but who I had helped to hang on to the sumptuous family home he occupied but couldn't really afford. Thus I thought he considered me a friend. Can you really believe it? With friends like this who needs enemies? So I kicked Lesley out of the house. Did you hear that? Doesn't sound like much does it? And if it's not happening to you it isn't much. But we had been together for thirty-three years. And then we weren't. I don't think it takes a massive imagination to understand what a huge trauma it is to split from your life partner of thirty-three years. Emotionally it's totally devastating. Or at least it was to me. So to cut a long story short, we lost the marriage, lost the house and neither of us was in the best of health to deal with all the inevitable, tears, heartache and confusion (or was that just me?) There were times when we were both in different hospitals having treatments at the same time. That's what I mean by a triple whammy. Health, finances and emotional security, all gone. A lifetime's work, gone. I was scraping along the very bottom. Trawling the depths of the deepest ocean. Low as you can go. I don't think you can go any lower and stay alive. Like I said, when people hear my story they often remark they're surprised I'm still standing. So how did I survive? Why am I not just still standing but stronger and better than ever before? The answer is by using the very methods I put forward here. When I had excruciating pain from the ulcer in the middle of the night they gave me liquid morphine and I was swigging it back like there was no tomorrow, hardly touched the blinking sides, but it made no difference. It actually seemed to make the pain worse at times. I took other powerful drugs and they hardly worked either. But the only thing that did work was a simple, psych-sensory pain relief method I had learned many years before on one of the hundreds of courses I attended and which I had used successfully with many clients. It was the only thing that kept me sane during that harrowing period. When I was depressed it was tapping and self-hypnosis that kept me sane and boosted my mood. When I needed to move on it was a combination of many of my techniques including breathing exercises and NLP that gave me the confidence to do so.

After Lesley and I split up I was naturally depressed. I don't think I realised at the time how low I was and when that happens you don't really know what to do or where to go. After a lifetime of work, creating a family, travelling far and wide and having amazing experiences of different kinds and always being in control of my destiny (or so I thought) I was at a loss to work out what should come next. After weighing up all the options I decided to return to my roots. My home town. So I arrived back in London at the age of sixty completely alone and stony broke. It's curious to note that even after twenty-four years of living in Ross-on-Wye the streets of North West London felt more like home than the streets of Herefordshire had ever done. Our family home out in those sticks for those years had been a very large, detached, Victorian house with a huge garden so I was used to lots of space. We had always loved that house and thought it was probably the last house either of us would live in. But now I was forced to exist in a tiny, one-bedroom apartment way up on the fourth floor where there wasn't enough room to swing a cat and I found it very difficult to adapt. At least I could shut the door and nobody could bother me. But these were not the ideal conditions in which to flourish and it was only hypnosis and the other techniques I've learned over the years and used to help others in dire straits that kept my head above water. Half way sane. That's how I know for sure that these things work because without them I might have given up completely. But of course, there was one other crucial ingredient that kept me going when the darkness was at its deepest and that of course was the unconditional love of my amazing kids who I have always loved more than anything. They are both successful and live abroad but always kept in touch to make sure I was okay. A few years later as my life gathered new momentum a wonderful thing happened. I was lucky enough to meet the most amazing person I had ever met in my life. But more to the point, we fell in love. Who would have thought it? I was daft enough to think that maybe romance might be over in my life but how wrong I was. Now I know that romance never dies. I had thought it was the end of the world but after the dust had settled and I regained my strength I realised it was the beginning of a new life. Not only had I survived the storm and just about everything they can throw at you but my life was now better than before. If I was religious I'd probably say it was some kind of a miracle. So that leads us to the moral of the story which, like all the best things in life, is very simple. You can do anything you want if you believe you can. Believe in yourself at all times. Never, never give up no matter how bad things seem to be or how low you feel. And you must love everyone as much as you can. Oh yes, and carry out the techniques I'm giving you here because they will help you just like they helped me even if you don't have any serious conditions.

Exercise 20 - Instant Pain Relief Method

This is the method I used when I was in excruciating pain from a stomach ulcer. It was the only thing that worked including drugs like morphine. Use this on yourself or with clients.

Take a nice big deep breath, hold it, breath out and relax.

Check the level of pain on a scale of 1-10.

Repeat these words aloud if possible

I'm calm and relaxed.

I wish to be free from pain.

I wish my left leg (or whatever's hurting) to be comfortable.

I wish my left leg to be supple.

I wish my left leg to be healthy and strong.

Now I'm going to ask you a question and there's only one answer to the question and the answer is yes. I hope that's okay.

And the question is: Do you wish to obtain psychological anaesthesia for your pain?

Say yes. Great, that's perfect.

Now I'd like you to make your mouth as moist as possible. Build up lots of saliva in your mouth.

More saliva than usual. Make your mouth nice and moist with saliva.

Good, now repeat the following words: My left leg is anaesthetised and comfortable.

That's it, your leg is now free from pain.

Check level of pain from 1-10 and how much it has gone down.

Most pain usually goes first time round but sometimes it can take a few times to get rid of it all.

Subjects often report they felt the affected area becoming warm and clammy during the process.

Fabulous Foxes

'It gives hope to all the young players out there who have been told they are not good enough. What do you need to arrive? A big name? A big contract? No. You just need to keep an open mind, an open heart, a full battery and run free.' - Claudio Ranieri

A few years ago Leicester City Football Club won the English Premier League. If you don't know much about football this won't mean much but if you do it means a lot. It was a stupendous achievement that lead to widespread comments in the football world roughly along the lines of 'How the blinking hell did they do that?' Because this was quite simply a miracle. It could not have come about without divine intervention.

The English Premiership is largely regarded as the best football league in the world attracting many of the world's finest and most expensive players. In recent times the winners have come from a select band of clubs namely Manchester United, Manchester City and Chelsea albeit closing in on them fast are Liverpool, Tottenham Hotspur and Arsenal. Only one of those six teams would be considered by most football fans as being possible championship contenders because they are quite simply the biggest and wealthiest in the land. Each has a massive squad of high quality international players to the point where they could field two entire teams of top international players. In 2015, the year Leicester City invoked a witch-doctor's spell and somehow managed to win the league their transfer spending on players was £52 million. A huge amount of money but dwarfed in comparison to the big boys - Manchester City £400 million, Manchester United £390 million and Chelsea £300 million. Now at this point you could quite justifiably ask what kind of society lavishes this kind of wealth on buying footballers (who all earn millions themselves besides these transfer values) when there is massive child poverty, food banks, falling down schools, a crumbling health service etc. And of course the answer you get from ardent capitalists is that our system may not be perfect but is the best anyone has invented so far. My response to them would be that it is high time we invented a better one but leaving that argument aside for the moment let's see if we can understand how on earth Leicester won the title against all the odds and all the tenets of capitalism which would dictate that the more you spend the better your chance of winning. Throughout the season, even towards the end of it, the Foxes, as they are known, continued to maintain their surprising lead at the top and during this time most of the most knowledgeable football pundits in the land (who in actual fact are only about as knowledgeable as the rest of us and maybe less) continued to insist that Leicester City could not and would not win the title. It had been a great effort, a delicious prospect, a tantalising dream but it was bound to come crashing down to earth very soon. They could not keep it up. Of course not. They didn't have the players or the expertise or the skill or the mental strength. The whole thing was a ridiculous fluke. Very soon order would be restored and something was bound to happen to put them in their place much further down the table. But no! On and on they went with amazing victory after amazing victory. Mouths were agape and pundits silenced as they drew closer and closer to their incredible prize with every match. They were focussed, they believed it and they did it. Without anywhere near the best players or anywhere near the best team, against all the odds and all the perceived wisdom, they won. So, let's ask again. How the blinking heck did they do it?

Clearly, without any doubt all it was because of their inspirational manager Claudio Ranieri. In raising the mental attitude, focus, belief and application of the team he lifted them above what anyone could have expected. By enhancing what I would call the psychic energy of the team it enabled the individual players and the team as a whole to do more, run further, tackle harder and generally lift performance levels to new heights. This is something all teams can do but the mental side of things is largely neglected by managers because they simply do not understand it. Claudio Ranieri found a way to transfer his own inspirational mind-set into the minds of his players so that they took to the field for every match in a totally positive state expecting to win. At the fourteen professional clubs where I have worked either with individual players or the team as a whole it is only when matters have deteriorated to a level seemingly beyond the manager's control that I have been given a chance to help and in every case performances and results have improved quite significantly.

Ranieri's wonderful success ranks as one of the greatest achievements ever in football. It was a moment of pure magic similar to Roger Bannister's sub four-minute mile when special people find extraordinary ways to achieve great things. It was a testament to the great things that can be achieved with a positive mental attitude which is exactly what my work is all about too. Claudio was lauded by everyone in football and just about every other sport too. The entire population of the city of Leicester which doesn't always have such a lot to shout about found itself with a great deal to shout about now. And it did. The feeling generated by this was one of great love for the manager and the team. However, such are the vagaries of the football world that half way through the next season, due to a run of poor results, Ranieri was unceremoniously sacked by the club. In my opinion they should have given him a job for life.

Exercise 21 - Stimulating the Sore Spots

The sore spots are located on either side of the chest. To find them you can spread your arms out wide and then fold inwards from the elbow. Your fingers should then be in touching distance of the sore spots which feel a bit like holes in the chest and are sensitive to the touch. Feel around a bit and you'll know when you've found them. The sore spots are connected to the lymphatic system which is part of the vascular system and an important part of the immune system, comprising a large network of lymphatic vessels that carry a clear fluid called lymph directionally towards the heart. As such it extends to many parts of the body and to many of its organs. This is incredibly easy. By using fingers to apply pressure to these spots or by massaging them you will feel stress and anxiety simply flowing away from you.

This is a very simple exercise you can use anywhere at any time to relax and get a nice boost to help you whatever you are doing.

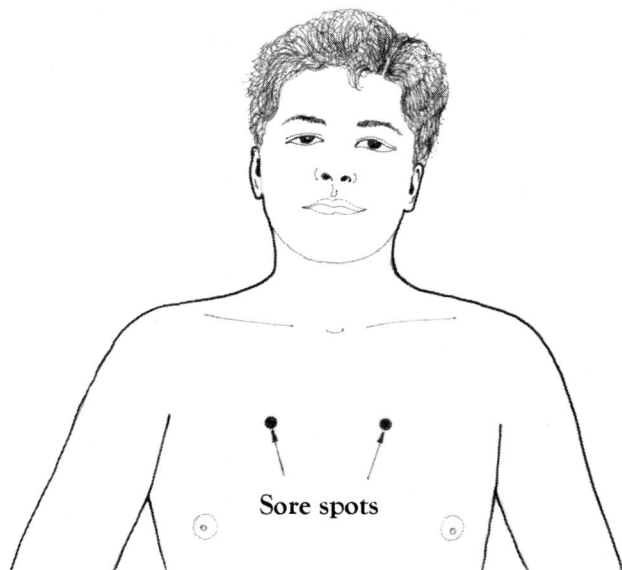

Sore spots

Einstein or Not

The following is a letter purporting to be from Albert Einstein to his daughter Lieserl. It is one of 1,400 letters written by Einstein that she donated to the Hebrew University in Jerusalem with instructions not to publish their contents until two years after his death. However, after various investigations there is now significant doubt if this letter was actually written by Einstein. Whether it was or not the letter is a beautiful read and whoever wrote it, it is very much in keeping with the sentiments of this book and therefore well worth an outing here. By the way, it's worth remembering at this point that Einstein formulated the theory of relativity while in a hypnotic trance.

'When I proposed the theory of relativity, very few understood me, and what I will reveal now to transmit to mankind will also collide with the misunderstanding and prejudice in the world.

I ask you to guard the letters as long as necessary, years, decades, until society is advanced enough to accept what I will explain below. There is an extremely powerful force that, so far, science has not found a formal explanation to. It is a force that includes and governs all others, and is even behind any phenomenon operating in the universe and has not yet been identified by us.

This universal force is LOVE. When scientists looked for a unified theory of the universe they forgot the most powerful unseen force. Love is Light, that enlightens those who give and receive it. Love is gravity, because it makes some people feel attracted to others.

Love is power, because it multiplies the best we have, and allows humanity not to be extinguished in their blind selfishness. Love unfolds and reveals.

For love we live and die. Love is God and God is Love.

This force explains everything and gives meaning to life. This is the variable that we have ignored for too long, maybe because we are afraid of love because it is the only energy in the universe that man has not learned to drive at will.

To give visibility to love, I made a simple substitution in my most famous equation. If instead of $E = mc^2$, we accept that the energy to heal the world can be obtained through love multiplied by the speed of light squared, we arrive at the conclusion that love is the most powerful force there is, because it has no limits.

After the failure of humanity in the use and control of the other forces of the universe that have turned against us, it is urgent that we nourish ourselves with another kind of energy...

If we want our species to survive, if we are to find meaning in life, if we want to save the world and every sentient being that inhabits it, love is the one and only answer.

Perhaps we are not yet ready to make a bomb of love, a device powerful enough to entirely destroy the hate, selfishness and greed that devastate the planet.

However, each individual carries within them a small but powerful generator of love whose energy is waiting to be released. When we learn to give and receive this universal energy, dear Lieserl, we will have affirmed that love conquers all, is able to transcend everything and anything, because love is the quintessence of life.

I deeply regret not having been able to express what is in my heart, which has quietly beaten for you all my life. Maybe it's too late to apologize, but as time is relative, I need to tell you that I love you and thanks to you I have reached the ultimate answer! ".

Your father Albert Einstein

Keystone Cops Therapy

'The pellet with the poison's in the vessel with the pestle, the chalice from the palace has the brew that is true.' - Spoken by Danny Kaye in the film The Court Jester

There's a paradox here and it's a great idea to get it out into the open so that nobody labours under any illusions. It's about hypnosis. Now there are many methods and practices that people turn to when they're in trouble with stress, anxiety, depression, falling short of ambitions etc. or when ambitious people want to improve their performance level in different ways such as athletes, business folk, performers, actors, dancers, singers etc. But when the best method of all, hypnosis, is put forward as a possible way to achieve their dreams and aspirations many of them tend to avoid it like the plague because, without wishing to put too fine a point on it, it scares them. Their main trepidation, and possibly their only trepidation, is that they don't like to lose control. Somehow they have adopted the strange idea that when you enter a hypnotic trance you lose control of your mind and the very idea scares the pants right off them. Happily then, I can confirm unequivocally that this is completely incorrect. Lose control in hypnosis? Absolutely not. Indeed, you gain control of your life like never before. You see things with a new sharpness. With the focus of a laser beam. And thus a paradox is created which is twofold. Firstly, you don't lose control. I think I said this already.

In a hypnotherapy session you are always in control of the whole process. You can get up and walk out of the room anytime you want to. But you don't want to because the experience is so great, enjoyable, effective, inspirational etc. But you can. Secondly, by avoiding hypnosis you spurn your very best way of achieving what you want to achieve because it is the very method that will help you above all other methods. It is a real shame. A paradox, a paradox, a most ingenious paradox, a ha ha ha ha ha ha ha, a paradox (thank you Gilbert and Sullivan).

There is a massive industry of corporate and so-called life coaching mostly executed by nitwits who have glittering certificates on their office walls but haven't got a clue what they're doing. Some of them use a little NLP (Neuro Linguistic Programming) but no hypnosis. Most of them don't even have the vaguest notion that NLP is a modality created by two hypnotists, Richard Bandler and John Grinder, and is itself a form of hypnosis. I know this because I've asked many of them. Richard Bandler has often been referred to as the best hypnotist in the world and is a genius in the field. All he does is hypnosis. Even at NLP events where he demonstrates his expertise, all he does is hypnosis and it's always a joy to observe even though he himself can be a bit surly. Those who know him will understand what I mean by this. But if you ask a life coach why they don't use hypnosis they have no answer because they've done a course in coaching and follow to the letter only what they have learnt by rote. They fiddle around on the edges of issues without really understanding them and are much more in need of help than those they are supposedly coaching. It's keystone cops therapy because in my opinion you simply cannot do the job of helping or coaching people properly without using hypnosis to one degree or another. Here you might think I'm only saying that because I am a hypnotist but it is the other way around. I am principally a hypnotist because I have discovered its amazing effectiveness. There is nothing to stop me using any other method and describing myself as a practitioner of that method but I am clear that hypnosis is the central theme of my work. Yes it is true that I use many other modalities to augment and strengthen the hypnosis but in a eureka moment many years ago I realised that in order to influence the mind of any subject in a positive way, whether an athlete, performer, business leader or anyone else you can think of, you have to communicate with the subconscious mind and life coaching or indeed sports psychology doesn't do that. Hypnosis does. Indeed, that's exactly what hypnosis does. If you told me I could only use one modality in my work then I would unequivocally choose hypnosis. That's it. Full stop. End of story. Say no more. Get it? Got it? Good.

The point I make is that the very best method available to help people achieve great things and be fulfilled in their lives is the very method they avoid like the plague and invent bogus reasons not to use. That's it. That's the paradox. Pity.

The sub-conscious mind or unconscious mind as it is sometimes referred to is where your behaviour patterns are created. They say it constitutes about 90% of your mind. It is the right-hand side of your mind. The subconscious is completely uncritical so it believes anything you tell it. Whatever you think or imagine travels along neural pathways into your unconscious mind which doesn't differentiate between what's real and what's imagined. So if, for instance, you visualise scoring great goals or winning tournaments or signing big contracts or singing perfectly in tune in front of thousands or dancing a difficult ballet perfectly at the Albert Hall or performing any discipline to a world class standard it registers that it's true, that you have actually done that thing and of course if you've done it once you can do it again. This gives you excellent confidence. That's why visualisation is such a great technique to use in sport or anything else even when carried out in the waking state. But it is a thousand times better, stronger and more potent if you carry it out in a hypnotic trance. This can be done in a hetero-hypnosis session (a session conducted by a hypnotist/hypnotherapist) or using self-hypnosis of which there is an explanation elsewhere in the book. Either way, I recommend it wholeheartedly.

Exercise 22 - Tracing the Lemniscate

The Lemniscate or the eight on its side is the mathematical symbol of infinity. Others see it as a symbol of the fact that we are eternal, limitless, and all connected.

Trace the Pattern of the lemniscate on your forehead to achieve deep relaxation very rapidly.

By doing this we are stimulating the third eye spot which activates the pituitary and pineal glands resulting in the release of oxytocin. Oxytocin is the antidote to the stress chemical cortisone and cancels it out completely.

This is an incredibly simple technique for eliminating stress and I cannot think of any reason at all not to use it.

It is perfectly safe and suitable to soothe a crying baby so all you young parents out there can now get a decent night's sleep. Use it on the baby then use it on yourself. It's a win, win.

Lemniscate pattern

War on Weight

'I can resist everything except temptation.' - Oscar Wilde

I often say that if you want to lose weight you need to close your mouth and move your ass. It really isn't rocket science. Eat less, get more exercise and just watch those pounds melt away. I know, easier said than done. It's a bloody nuisance isn't it? All the food we like best, Indian, Chinese, pizzas, bacon sandwiches, fried meat of any kind, fish & chips, chips by themselves, more chips, sticky toffee pudding, ice cream etc. are the very worst things we can put into our bodies. Clogging up the arteries, piling on the pounds, fomenting unsociable odours that disgorge from every orifice, creating all kinds of embarrassing health issues. But if you use the methods I set out here you will be able to resist all those nefarious substances that surround us 24/7 so that in the future you will glow with good health and be perfectly satisfied just licking a postage stamp and washing it down with a glass of warm water. (only kidding).

Here are a few tips to assist in the process of resisting those naughty temptations and sticking much more to leafy, green vegetables, wholegrain bread and pasta, lean meat and fish etc. Of course you don't have to be an absolute saint about this. The main thing is to eat much less, stick to the healthy stuff as far as possible and be proud of yourself for doing so. And I certainly don't mean going on a starvation diet because then you can easily slip into the troglodyte mentality of our ancestors that lurks in our paleo-ancestral memory. In those days long ago when dinosaurs roamed the earth, we were all hunter gatherers lurching about in our tribes, much as football supporters do now, searching for food. But unlike football fans, there were not grocery stores every ten yards to buy a meat pie and a fizzy drink or a pub where we could sip a pint (or two) or a chippie, pizza place or Chinese takeaway to soak up the alcohol. What happened was that every now and again we would club together and manage to kill an animal of some sort then gorge on the carcass and swallow down as much as we possibly could because we had no idea when the next brontosaurus would be along. That's the frame of mind we enter when we starve ourselves to lose weight so that after a few days we just want to devour any kind of food we can get our hands on, particularly the more unhealthy kind. We end up putting on more pounds that we took off by starving ourselves. It's one reason why diets don't work.

If you can give up meat then I advise you very strongly to do so because it takes much longer to pass through the system and this possibly causes disease. It is certainly the case that in countries where they eat less meat, for instance Japan, they have less bowel cancer. Also, we now know that animals, particularly cows, emit great quantities of methane into the atmosphere which is harmful to the environment. Actually, thinking about it, I have quite a few mates who do that too. But you wouldn't want to eat them. A glance would put you right off. The point is that we manufacture cows and other animals for the food market and this contributes a huge amount to greenhouse gases that are destroying the environment. Methane is more harmful even than carbon dioxide. I have not eaten meat for most of my adult life and I can tell you it's a very easy thing to do. You feel much better and lighter knowing that you are healthier and not contributing to the appalling animal cruelty which is very widespread and harms our souls terribly.

'Nothing will benefit human health and increase chances for survival of life on earth as much as the evolution to a vegetarian diet.' Albert Einstein (Nobel Prize 1921).

Now for some practical suggestions for losing weight.

Drink a pint of water before every meal. This makes you feel quite full with a substance that has no calories before you even start eating so that you feel more full up much quicker whilst eating less food.

Use small plates such as a side plate instead of a dinner plate. This is because after the meal your unconscious mind registers that you have eaten a whole plate of food, whatever the size, and sends the full up signal to the stomach even though you have only eaten half as much food as usual.

Sniff vanilla essence. Yes that's right. A special trick of mine that I've been giving to clients for many years and it works incredibly well. It is easily available so carry a small container round with you wherever you go and take regular sniffs particularly before any meals or snacks. This suppresses your appetite so you eat much less. Didn't know that did you?

Enjoy feeling hungry. Yes, enjoy that empty feeling knowing that it is doing you good. Get to really enjoy that hungry sensation because it is helping you do something you couldn't do before. But you can now, right? Because you just love that hungry feeling.

Think of a type of food you really don't like. Something that makes you sick to your stomach. Next time you're faced with a large plate of unhealthy food or you find yourself with your nose pressed up against the window of a fast food outlet achingly tempted by the luscious, greasy, fried meaty offerings inside then do this. Imagine all that tempting, unhealthy food mixed up together with the food you don't like, the food that turns your stomach and it will put you right off eating it. If you haven't got a particular food that creates this bilious effect then imagine mixing the tempting, unhealthy food with a bowl of sick or the sweepings of dust and hair from a barber's shop floor. Mix it all up together, imagine putting in your mouth and swallowing it down and see how much of it you feel like eating now!

Here's another way to do it. Think of an unhealthy food you can't stop eating. Kebabs, chips, pizzas, ice cream etc. Imagine

Eating the food and swallowing it down and notice how it tastes. Now tap on your collarbone as per the tapping points diagram elsewhere in the book. Again imagine eating some of that same food, chewing it and swallowing it down. Notice how it tastes now. The same or maybe less tasty? Now tap on the under eye point, the under arm point and the collarbone again. Tap on the third eye point. Check how the food tastes. By now it will probably not taste so nice. Now go through the whole 9-gamut process described on page 59. Check how the food tastes. After a while tapping in this sequence, longer for some than others, the food will usually lose its flavour altogether then begin to taste quite awful and you will lose interest in eating it at all. This might be straight away or after a few rounds of tapping. The loss of flavour may or may not happen first but after a short while the taste of the food will change to bland, then nasty then disgusting and worse. It will taste such that you will lose interest in ever eating it again. As I have already said, no two people are the same and there can be different reactions to these techniques so in some cases this effect will happen straight away and in some cases it will take a bit longer. If desire for the tempting, unhealthy kind of food creeps back at any stage in the future just repeat the exercise and take it away again. Having already gone through the process it should now work just as well by simply by tapping the collarbone alone (see diagram on page 131). Just a quick warning though. This exercise can be so potent that people have been known to gag while doing it. I have seen it happen.

And now, another way to do it. Follow the self-hypnosis instructions and when you get to the part where you introduce affirmations say to yourself things like 'Unhealthy food is of no interest to me. I don't like fried food, chips and pizzas. Once I enjoyed it but now it has no power over me anymore. I enjoy healthy fresh food. I enjoy green vegetables and lean fish. I can lose weight and I am losing weight. From this moment on I eat less and exercise more and I lose weight every day.' You get the gist don't you? Make up your own affirmations, words that mean something to you. Keep it positive and in the present tense for about ten minutes then count yourself up and notice the changes. Do this regularly.

Use the control room technique (exercise 8). Turn down the dial that controls your desire to eat any unhealthy, fatty foods and turn up the control for healthy foods. Turn down the hunger dial too. Make sure to take the hot button with you so you can control these things with a simple touch wherever you go.

If you need more help, feel free to get in touch.

Thank You For Smoking

'Giving up smoking is the easiest thing in the world. I know because I've done it thousands of times.' - Mark Twain

First of all, and let's be absolutely clear about this, there are no advantages to smoking. None at all. I know some people say it de-stresses them but this is incorrect. In fact, the opposite is the case. Smoking increases the heart rate so it makes you even more stressed. I don't think I'm breaking confidence with any professional ethics here when I say that regular smokers are addicted to nicotine, one of the many nefarious, carcinogenic substances contained in tobacco. There are over eighty such substances in a cigarette but nicotine is probably the most potent. They say a single drop could kill a horse. What happens when you smoke is that you are feeding your addiction to nicotine and that makes you feel more comfortable. This is the state that some smokers confuse with de-stressing. It's like a junkie getting his fix. The de-stressing misnomer is merely an excuse for partaking in this guilty pleasure that we all know is incredibly bad for us and everyone around us. For instance, those who have to ingest the secondary smoke, smell the stale, pungent breath, watch the uncomfortable wheezing of the smoker climbing the stairs, see the leathery, nicotine-stained teeth and unhealthy pallor of the smoke ravaged face etc. Like I said, no advantages at all. Some smoke because they enjoy it and say they don't want to give up. Well I guess you can't save everyone and if people really want to puff their lives away then that is up to them. I was once standing next to a guy at a railway station who couldn't get his lighter going. He was getting really annoyed he couldn't light his cigarette.

'Good time to quit.' I said.

'But I've only just started.' He replied.

However, polls show that the majority of about ten million smokers in the UK and about forty million in the US would like to give it up. Some just don't know how to quit whilst others find it too daunting a prospect. But if you really want to stop this dangerous habit then there is hope and I can tell you from personal experience that it is not as difficult as you think. You can do it now, in a second. Just make the decision and stick to it. The easiest way is to simply stop buying cigarettes and go cold turkey. You may experience some withdrawal effects for two or three days but it won't kill you and on the contrary it may save your life. Keep encouraging yourself through the process by saying things like 'I can quit smoking and I will quit smoking. It's going to feel so great to be a non-smoker.' With every couple of hours that pass congratulate yourself. Say 'Well done mate. Your willpower is strong. Your determination is strong. You can do this.' Feel proud of yourself as each non-smoking day goes by. Eventually you reach that magical moment when you realise you've done it. It's a truly great feeling and worth everything it takes to get there. For many this is enough to get through the process. However, if you experience problems with this approach then you may need some help. Unfortunately however, not all the help offered is much good however well-meaning it may be. In the UK all doctor's surgeries provide advice and help by way of patches, chewing gum or tablets called Zydol. The patches and gum are nicotine replacement therapy. The idea is that they feed nicotine into the system so that you don't feel any withdrawal symptoms when you stop smoking. The problem is that you remain addicted to nicotine and sooner or later you'll probably start smoking again. As far as the tablets are concerned, if you read the list of their possible side effects such as sickness, diarrhoea, dizziness etc. you might easily decide that smoking is a preferable option. But the main problem with these methods is much more basic. They don't work. Statistics show that the success level of all the stop-smoking devices handed out by UK doctor surgeries is a miniscule six percent. Against this the success of hypnotherapy in stopping people smoking is a whopping eighty-five percent. In other words we are regularly wasting huge amounts of money on methods that don't work whilst deliberately spurning a method that does. This is because the current UK government has almost completely purged complementary methods from the NHS. This myopic approach is not only a great shame but also a huge mistake. I have approached a number of GP surgeries and Members of Parliament with a plan to carry out group stop smoking sessions. Yes, you can do it in a group. Over the years I have run hundreds of group hypnosis sessions for various issues and they are always invigorating, inspirational and successful in their purpose. Statistics show that out of a hundred people in a group stop- smoking session eighty-five will succeed in quitting there and then. If you charged £20 each it makes the whole exercise self-funding so a great saving for public funds. At this point I should state that I believe totally in the principle tenet of the NHS to provide health care free of charge at the point of delivery. However, smokers on twenty cigarettes a day are spending about three thousand pounds a year on their useless, unhealthy habit so in this case I think it is perfectly fair to charge a modest fee because they will save a great deal of money on the deal. And very likely their life too. Also, the NHS will save huge amounts not having to treat them later in life for any of the smoking-related diseases such as lung cancer. The current cost of smoking-related healthcare is estimated at between two and five billion pounds a year. Of course, it may not be entirely unfair to expect a contribution from tobacco companies who make big profits and pay little tax. After all, it is their product that causes the problem.

Some don't want to quit because they think they'll gain weight. What nonsense is this? Are they really prepared to get bronchitis, emphysema, lung cancer, heart disease just for the sake of looking slim? Let me tell you that these two things are not mutually exclusive. You can quite easily quit smoking and stay slim and millions have. Every packet of cigarettes sold in the UK has quite a large notice printed on it saying in no uncertain terms words that 'If you smoke these it will probably kill you'. Smoking a cigarette after reading this is akin to walking blind-folded across a busy main road. You may be very lucky and survive but statistics are against it. Of course what the tobacco companies are keen for you to do is take up vaping because that's where all their investment is directed these days and they have even persuaded a UK governmental, all-party committee to make it a policy to recommend vaping over smoking. These companies still push their lethal tobacco products hard in under-developed countries where sales are booming but in the western world where people are now wise to the disastrous effects of smoking they are switching their efforts to this new product they claim is safe. But they can't prove it's safe and in fact nobody knows what the long-term effects of vaping actually are. Remember, tobacco companies promoted smoking cigarettes as a healthy pastime for many years. Those of us of a certain age will remember the 'Come to Marlboro country.' Advert on TV and at the cinema which depicted a hunky, very fit and attractive looking cowboy sitting on a similarly hunky, very fit and attractive looking horse in a beautiful country landscape replete with river, trees and mountains. The cowboy was of course smoking his head off not to mention smiling his daft ass off. Obviously this was all designed to establish a phoney association between smoking and a wholesome lifestyle. How gullible must we all have been? I'll bet after filming the poor horse coughed its lungs up all over the set. But it isn't just the smokers or vapers who are prone to the lethal conditions and diseases of smoking. It is also the people nearby who are forced to ingest the toxic smoke that billows from those little machines. Have you seen how it blows out like a steam train enveloping everything in the vicinity? However pleasant they make the description of the flavours of those things - blueberry, watermelon, lemonade, strawberry, banana custard, blueberry cheesecake (who are they kidding?) does not mask the deadly possibilities they may represent. It was years before the extreme dangers of cigarettes were known and the dangers of vaping are still not known. So it's up to you my friends to decide if that's a risk you wish to take or not. The point to bear in mind is that commercial interests are ruthless and do not coincide with the health interests of the public at large.

Other ways to stop are as follows:

Say to yourself I can quit and I have quit. Keep saying it to yourself. Also say things like cigarettes have no power over me anymore. I have no need of cigarettes. Cigarettes are a thing of the past etc. Make up your own affirmations and make sure they are strong and positive.

Carry out the Happy Tapping procedure from exercise 3 and replace the wording with 'I want to quit smoking, I can quit smoking, I will quit smoking, I have quit smoking, I'm okay. Then for the second part say 'I want to be even healthier, I can be even healthier, I will be even healthier, I am even healthier because I have given up smoking. I'm okay, I'm more than okay.

Imagine unwrapping a new pack of cigarettes, removing the silver paper and taking out a cigarette. Imagine putting it in your mouth and taking a big drag. Notice how the smoke tastes. Now tap on either collarbone point (see diagram page 131) about twenty times and then imagine taking another big drag. How does it taste now? Usually there is a difference and sometimes a big difference. It might start tasting of nothing or start tasting disgusting. Go through the 9-gamut process (exercise 7), Imagine another drag on the cigarette and check again how it tastes. By this time the taste can be completely horrible. It can take a few rounds of this type of tapping to get to this point or it may happen straight away.

By doing this procedure some begin to gag at the very thought of smoking and feel physically sick to their stomach. Like all these exercises, some have a more extreme reaction than others. If it doesn't immediately occur as described keep going with the exercise until it does. After this, if you are tempted to smoke at any time you should be able to merely tap on the collarbone point to bring back those nauseating feelings about smoking and the temptation will pass.

Enter the control room of your mind (exercise 8) and turn the dial that controls your desire to smoke right down to the lowest level. You can even switch it right off and see the light go out as you do. Take the hot button with you everywhere in case any desire to smoke creeps in. Touch the hot button and feel it disappear.

Follow the self-hypnosis procedure (exercise 14) and when you're nicely and deeply relaxed bring all those positive affirmations to mind and say them to yourself. 'I am a non-smoker. I am a clean air breather. Smoking is of no interest to me anymore. I can quit and I have quit.' Etc. make up other affirmations that mean something to you such as maybe 'My kids are proud of me because I have giving up smoking'. Take your time over this and spend at least twenty minutes on this method. As with weight loss, if you need more help please get in touch. But if you really want to quit you should now be able to do it entirely by yourself using these methods. Promise. Please let me know how you get on.

Conclusion

Let me end with the same simple, heartfelt message I started with and which I have been pounding into your head ever since. That there are a number of simple, rapid, potent techniques that anyone can easily learn and if you do them every day you will feel better, function better, be happier and improve every aspect of your life. Guaranteed. They are here in this book so no excuses. Now is the time. Now is always the time. Yes I know, repeating myself again but with the purest of intentions I assure you. As you finish reading this book I do sincerely hope that these words will ring in your ears, echo in your mind and vibrate in your heart because then we can go forward together and make the world a happier place. I also hope you haven't just turned to this page hoping for a funny punch line because I'd prefer you to read the whole thing if you wouldn't mind. I will even come round to your house and read it to you if you like.

So in conclusion I think I'll leave the very last words to that gentle and enlightened soul, Bertrand Russell who I have already quoted earlier in this tome and whose words I urge everyone to read and consider.

'I believe in using words, not fists. I believe in my outrage knowing people are living in boxes on the street. I believe in honesty. I believe in a good time. I believe in good food. I believe in sex.' - Bertrand Russell

Keep smiling everybody, Peter